D1196292

AMERICAN CLASSICS

The Acquisition of Political, Social, and Industrial Rights of Man in America

JOHN BACH McMASTER

With an introduction by
LOUIS FILLER
Antioch College

FREDERICK UNGAR PUBLISHING CO.
NEW YORK

Printed in the United States of America

Library of Congress Catalog Card No. 61-18663

JOHN BACH McMASTER
Historian of Democracy

When McMaster in 1883 published his first volume of *A History of the People of the United States*, he created one of the literary sensations of the year. His book appealed not only to historians, who hastened to recognize a major achievement in their field, but to the general reading public as well. McMaster was then thirty-one years of age, and an instructor in geodesy, a branch of mathematics, at what became Princeton University. He had already published two small technical books; but he had also long indulged a deep enthusiasm for American history. This impelled him to pore over old papers, old books, and old pamphlets in the Astor Library of his native New York and elsewhere. Out of these—and his reading in the English historian, Macaulay, among others— he had conceived the idea of a new American history. It would not merely dramatize its heroes and national crises, in the style of George Bancroft, it would do more than record events, as Richard Hildreth was so often prone to do. In the dusty ephemera which he consulted, McMaster found record of matters which had hitherto seemed unworthy of note by historians of stature and pretention, but which McMaster found fascinating: common occurrences, popular trends and fashions, and forgotten controversies and controversialists.

Introduction

In the *Gazette of the United States*, in the *New York Packet*, in the *American Museum*, and many other periodicals, in old memoirs and biographies, historical society papers, and official journals and debates he found references to matters which his readers agreed were intensely interesting and illuminating. How had letter-writing been conducted, in the early days of the Republic? It appeared that many people, especially those engaged in serious and responsible communication, had written in cipher to frustrate curious stage-coach carriers. There had been vigorous opposition to the theater in Philadelphia, Boston, and New York. Then, as later, maidservants married and had to be replaced. Counterfeiters had been busy in 1784. Noah Webster's attempts to reform spelling had been argued back and forth with partisan resourcefulness. Only the rich had enjoyed oranges and bananas, and the cauliflower and the eggplant had graced no dinner tables. Ice was rarely available for use out of season. Lotteries paid for everything from the building of a German Reformed Church in Maryland to the increasing of the library at Harvard College. The arrogance of the Barbary pirates was a matter of deep concern to American shippers. These, and a thousand other bits of data McMaster had jotted down in his notebooks, often with quotations from newspapers and magazines which were as fresh and inimitable as the day they had first been coined.

McMaster did not merely seek the odd and the unknown. He turned his attention on the new American nation and its leaders to report the organi-

Introduction

zation of the United States government, Shays's Rebellion in Massachusetts, and, in the 1790's, the differences developing between Jeffersonians and Hamiltonians, which turned bitter and dangerous in the red glare of the French Revolution. All this, too, he reported along with a stream of special information respecting the minting of American money, the origin of the song "Hail, Columbia," uncomplimentary opinions of President George Washington, the organization of Congress, and all manner of gossip and attitudes of the time.

With the success of what became volume one of his *History*, McMaster received an appointment of professor of American history at the University of Pennsylvania. There he continued industriously to collect materials for succeeding volumes. His story of what emphatically was a history of the *people* of the United States continued on through the stormy years of Jefferson's Administrations, it offered generous space to the unceasing expansion of Americans into the West, it took in the War of 1812, the Jacksonian "revolution," and the great struggles, entwined with foreign and domestic affairs, which embroiled North and South and carried American citizens to Mexico and to Oregon before the Civil War.

The almost popular interest and appreciation which attended the publication of volume one changed their content as new volumes followed after old. In 1913, McMaster published his eighth volume, which was concerned with the grim actions of pro-slavery and anti-slavery fighters, but also with the advent

Introduction

of Chinese immigrants, the panic of 1854, spiritualism, the Mormons, and the Pony Express. By that time, the *History of the People of the United States* seemed a monument of research which, though tersely and clearly-expressed, could only be handled with any degree of comfort by an expert. The ordinary reader could not presumably hope to approach it except by way of its index and for special research purposes.

Yet there was a thread which gave continuity to McMaster's forest of facts. McMaster had a vision of the American past which was vivid and compelling to him. The story of America he saw as one of a constantly evolving democracy. He was not only a pioneer of social history. He broke ground independently with his realistic concern for the detail of American freedoms. It did not suffice for him, as it did for so many other historians, that the Constitution of the United States had proclaimed individual rights. Volume one of his *History* had contributed pages lurid with facts regarding the infamous conditions of early American prisons. Volume two described, among other matters, the "terrors of the middle passage" from Africa to America which brought enslaved Negroes to our shores. Volume three noted the limited suffrage available to citizens. Volume four was especially strong in its awareness of the suffering caused by pauperism and the harsh effects of laws ordering imprisonment for debt. Though all these matters were set down with firm efforts at impartial recording, there could be no question but that McMaster

Introduction

deplored such traditions of injustice and lack of humanity in earlier America. A notable essay by him, originally published in the *Atlantic Monthly*[1], was entitled, "The Political Depravity of the Fathers."

Another, his official address as president of the American Historical Association was "Old Standards of Public Morals,"[2] which McMaster found reprehensible. It is not surprising that social-minded reformers of his time who had some awareness of American history should have been excited by his peremptory dismissal of sentimental views of the Founding Fathers and their work, and should have approved his impatience with accounts of them which took the "glittering generalities" of the Constitution as describing the real condition of the people. Life in early America, McMaster asserted, had been hard for large classes of its population. It had only been as a result of great efforts on the part of reformers, supported by needy and courageous elements of the community, that changes had been wrought.

All this McMaster was able to explain at length in the three extraordinary lectures which he delivered in the spring of 1903 at Western Reserve University in Cleveland, Ohio, under the auspices of the Daughters of the American Revolution. *The Acquisition of Political, Social and Industrial Rights of Man in America* once more presented McMaster in the role of a pioneer who rejected the fashionable notions of

[1]May, 1895, 626-633; reprinted in McMaster's *With the Fathers: Studies in the History of the United States* (New York, 1896), 71-86.

[2]*American Historical Review*, XI (April, 1906), 515-528.

Introduction

the past: of a happy and united people effortlessly creating a democratic society. On the contrary, his lectures emphasized, they had been divided by the realities of special privilege, by cruel legislation, and by bigoted assumptions. McMaster saw this condition as requiring historical perspective. Equal rights could not have been attained overnight and by fiat, he believed. Before industrial rights could be won, social rights had to be established. They, in turn, could not have been developed but for the political rights which had been won. The revolutionary fathers had had to proceed with moderation: "To have suddenly produced [a more equitable] social condition ... to have recklessly removed from the statute books every law ... would have been acts of disorganization of the worst kind."[3] McMaster saw the expansion of American democracy as an evolutionary development, as a product of experience and enlightenment. He had no fears that he was demeaning the nation or its leaders by reminding his auditors of its crude beginnings and tragic practice.

In his lectures, McMaster all but outlined the central theme of his *History*, a theme which wove through its first five volumes. *The Acquisition of the Political, Social and Industrial Rights of Man in America* concentrated a remarkable quantity of raw data, as well as interpretation, in its relatively brief compass. It offered nothing less than a key to the almost 3,000 pages of the *History's* first five volumes —a key which could enable not only the scholar, but

[3]See pages 40-41, in the following lectures.

Introduction

the general reader as well, to perceive McMaster's intent in the extended work. Here was his view of America's growth as a democracy. Hereafter, no reader would need to be daunted by the staggering proportions of McMaster's investigations, no reader would need to be bewildered by the *History's* torrents of facts and references.

Yet when the lectures were published in that same year of 1903, it was in an edition limited to no more than five hundred copies. These were quickly distributed and forgotten by all except specialists. Though their reviewer in the *American Historical Review* (October, 1904) wished that the volume "could be placed in the hands of every grammar-school and high-school teacher of American history," the lectures have been among the lost writings of American life and letters.

Analysts of McMaster's work have since noted discrepancies in his writings which might escape the less professional reader. In several cases they have sharply qualified his right to honor as a libertarian. They have found grounds for criticism even in his *History*, despite McMaster's praise for the democratic upsurges which had widened the suffrage (as exemplified by the Dorr War[4]), ended imprisonment for debt, produced institutional reforms, and finally ended slavery. They have observed that McMaster had not revealed himself as in sympathy with radicals, or even with all the "people" whose tale he had presumably intended to write. McMaster viewed

[4]For a summary, see pages 111 ff., in the ensuing lectures.

Introduction

mobs with suspicion. He was no admirer of Thomas Jefferson and Andrew Jackson. He regarded Irish and other immigrants with markedly less enthusiasm than he did persons of Anglo-Saxon descent. And while he praised the reformers of pre-Civil War decades for criticizing conservative upholders of the *status quo* and assaulting their institutions, he rejected the reformers of his very own time as cranks and worse. Students who were aware of the distraught conditions of American life in the 1880's and after— of hunger, unemployment, industrial warfare, desperation in cities and on the farm—could only wonder at his optimism. Despite the drastic depressions of 1883 and 1893, which dragged on for years, despite the Haymarket Riot of 1886, the Homestead and Pullman Strikes of the 1890's, and every type of disorder in between, McMaster felt free to sing the praises of American democracy and his devout faith in the reality of progress.[5]

[5]"As we have grown more intelligent, so we have grown more liberal, more tolerant, more humane. When this century opened there was not a blind asylum, nor a deaf and dumb asylum, nor a lunatic asylum, nor a house of refuge in all our land. We have turned our prisons from stews and brothels and seminaries of crime into reformatories of crime. We have cut down the number of crimes punished with death from fifteen to two. We have ceased to use the branding iron and the treadmill; we have abolished imprisonment for debt; we have exterminated slavery, and raised the laborer from a vassal to a man. We have covered our country with free schools and free libraries, and set up institutions for the protection not only of children but of dumb brutes. In the face of these facts it is wicked to talk of degeneration and decay," *With the Fathers*, 321.

Introduction

Yet the fact that McMaster was not interested in the reform needs of his own time—the fact that he had used the misery of the past as a foil for the alleged happiness of the present—did not impugn the validity of his analyses of the period with which his *History* dealt. One critic of McMaster complained that his *History* lacked "dynamic quality," and that this was the case because he had "hesitated to point his vast store of facts toward a conclusion."[6] As the following lectures amply demonstrate, McMaster did not at all fear to reach conclusions, and did not hesitate to affirm them without equivocation. McMaster was a man of courage and independence. What his critic failed to appreciate was that he was, simply, the complete historian, able to sit, read, and burden himself with notes, with the infinite patience that a man must have who has committed himself to decades of research. McMaster was not of the hypothesizers who hunt for bits of information which will seem to support their conjectures. He was a thoroughly absorbed scholar, who brought from his studies rich deposits of lore which he placed forthrightly before his readers. McMaster believed in the validity of the world he inhabited and the society he adorned; and perhaps it was just as well that he was an historian rather than a politician. But his prejudices, his view of America as a land of opportunity and healthy competition, the arbitrary nature of some of his

[6]William T. Hutchinson, "John Bach McMaster," in *The Marcus W. Jernegan Essays in American Historiography* (Chicago, 1937), 132.

Introduction

judgments, were transparently sincere, and he exercised his democratic rights in asserting them. No one in his time had better earned than McMaster the privilege of asserting that hard work and self-control must inevitably result in success for anyone. Thus, he exemplified in his own person and in his own achievement the democratic principles which his great *History* illustrated. He crystallized those principles in the following lectures. Students who have wished to understand our own times and to report them with persuasive accuracy and details, students who would wish to get behind the mask of wishful thinking, can learn much from McMaster's industry and respect for facts. These lectures can lead them to his *History*, and so to our own.

Louis Filler

Antioch College
Yellow Springs, Ohio
September, 1961

The Acquisition
of Political, Social,
and Industrial Rights
of Man in America

CONTENTS

LECTURE I

The Acquisition of the Political Social and Industrial Rights of Man in America.

The subject that I am to have the pleasure of presenting is " The Acquisition of the Political, Social, and Industrial Rights of Man."

It would seem to fall naturally into the three divisions mentioned, but in covering the period from the opening of the Revolution down to the middle of the nineteenth century neither one of these great struggles has been continuous. There have been periods of great activity, followed by periods of apparent indifference. I have thought it best, therefore, to present all three in the order in which they happen to fall chronologically.

You will recall that when the quarrel between the mother country and her rebellious colonies in America was brought to a crisis by the passage of the four intolerable acts, a congress of delegates gathered at Philadelphia to remonstrate against these acts of tyranny. You will recall that when these patriots had drawn up:

An address to the people of the colonies,
An address to the Carolinians,
An address to the people of Great Britain,
An address to the King,

and a long declaration of rights and grievances, they adjourned to meet again on the 10th of May, 1775. But when the 10th of May came, the colonists had ceased to remonstrate and had begun to fight; a shot heard round the world had been fired at Concord Bridge, and the country was ringing with the news that a gallant British army had been chased into Boston, and was there besieged by a band of minute men and militia encamped on the hills round about. By the mere force of circumstances then, this body of remonstrants, when they reassembled in Philadelphia, was forced to become a Continental Congress, and upon them was thrust the duty of conducting the country through the opening years of a great war.

The immediate results of this appeal to arms in Massachusetts was the final overthrow of all royal authority, and an appeal by the Provincial Congress of Massachusetts — which had assumed to assert all authority in Massachusetts — an appeal by it to the Continental Congress for advice. The letter sets forth that the trouble under which the colony labors for want of " regular government is serious, and asks Congress for explicit advice concerning the taking up and exercising of the powers of civil government,'' and pledges Massachusetts to submit to such a general plan as the Congress may direct for the colonies.

Congress answered that no obedience was due to the act of Parliament changing the charter of Massachusetts Bay, nor to a governor or lieutenant governor bent on subverting instead of obeying the charter; that these men were to be regarded as absent, and their offices looked upon as vacant; that the Provincial Congress should write to the towns entitled to representation urging them to choose members of the Assembly, which Assembly so chosen should elect a Council, and that these two bodies should exercise the powers of government until a governor of His Majesty's appointment would consent to govern according to the charter.

A few months later the delegates from New Hampshire presented a letter asking "for the advice and direction of Congress with respect to the method of administering justice and regulating our civil police." To this Congress replied recommending the Provincial Convention of New Hampshire "to call a full and free representation of the people, and that these representatives, if they think it necessary, establish such a form of government as in their judgment will best produce the happiness of the people."

On the following day, November 4, 1775, precisely the same advice in precisely the same words was given to South Carolina and, before the year closed, to Virginia. Early in 1776, some zealous whigs of New York wrote to John Adams asking that authority be given by Congress to New York to form a government. Moved it may well be by this appeal, Adams now submitted a resolution recommending that all the colonies be advised to form such governments as might be conducive to their happiness in particular, and to that of America in general.

The year which had now elapsed since the fight at Concord, had been fruitful of events which did much to strengthen the rising spirits of the colonists. The King on his part had declared his colonies to be in a state of rebellion; he had closed their ports to trade, had refused to receive their humble petitions, had sent ships and troops to subdue them, and had hired Hessians to aid him in this task. Congress, on its part, in ordinance after ordinance had assumed a sovereignty quite incompatible with the idea of allegiance to the King and Parliament. The little band of patriots gathered around Boston had been turned into the Continental Army and provided with a commander-in-chief. Letters of marque had been issued; the Tories had been disarmed, the ports had been thrown open to all nations, and a secret committee of correspondents were seeking assistance abroad. In the face of these facts it was idle to pretend that any allegiance was still due to the King. The resolution of Adams was therefore taken up and adopted, and on the 15th of May, 1776, a preamble was added in these words:

" Whereas, the King of Great Britain has excluded the colonies from protection of the crown, and given no answer to the humble petition for redress; and whereas the whole force of the King is to be used to the ruin of the colonies, it is absolutely inconceivable to reason and to conscience for the people now to take the oaths and affirmations to support any government under the crown; and it being necessary to suppress every kind of authority under the crown, therefore it is recommended to the assemblies and conventions of the United Colonies where no government sufficient for the exigencies of their affairs has been established, to adopt such government as shall in the opinion of the representatives of the people best conduce to the happiness of their constituents in particular and Americans in general."

But one thing, a formal declaration of independence, now remained to be done; and this Congress was not slow in doing it. June 7th Mr. Lee introduced his resolution declaring the United Colonies to be free and independent states. June 11th Congress appointed two committees, one to draft a declaration of independence, and one to frame a plan of general government for the republic about to be created. July 2nd the resolution of Lee was adopted and two days later the declaration which announced to the world the independence of the United States.

" A decent respect for the opinions of mankind," says the Declaration, " required that the causes which impelled our forefathers to the separation should be declared." But they went further than a mere statement of the specific acts of misgovernment by King and Parliament which led to this act of separation, and in that Declaration announced certain fundamental principles of government which they called self-evident truths.

Up to this point in the contest between the colonies and the mother country the colonies had taken their stand chiefly on constitutional grounds. They had asserted that their fathers had been English subjects; that in migrating to this country they had not gone without the realm and that they and their descendants remained English subjects; that one of the rights of an English subject was not to be taxed without representation; that it was impossible for them to be represented in Parliament, and therefore Parliament could not tax them. That ground had been answered and fairly well refuted, and in the Declaration of Independence the colonists shifted their ground from the old doctrine of the constitutional rights of the colonies to the theory which had been so popular in the early part of the century — the theory of Social Compact. Briefly stated that was: that before there was any civil government man existed in a state of nature; that in that state he was subject to natural laws and was possessed of a number of so-called natural rights; that as government had to be created, it was created by each individual yielding what he thought necessary for the good of all — that it was a social compact or contract in which each gave up enough of his natural rights to permit the establishment of organized authority; and that therefore when a government proved to be unsatisfactory the people had a natural right to alter or amend it. No man, it was further held, in this state of nature was subject to any other; that all men are equal, not physically or intellectually, but equal so far as concerns jurisdiction or authority; that no man is born to rule another. Natural rights then, are the basis of all political rights; our liberties do not come from charters nor from parchments nor from kings, but from the King of Kings.

What constituted these natural rights was then stated distinctly in the Declaration:

1. That all men are created equal.

2. All have been endowed by their Maker with certain inalienable rights of which they cannot be stripped by any power, and of which they cannot lawfully deprive themselves.

3. That among these rights are life, liberty and the pursuit of happiness.

If these are truths it follows that no government can claim allegiance or obedience from man unless he agrees to give it; that all government is a contract and that, in the words of the Declaration, " Government is constituted among men for the sole purpose of protecting these rights; " that all governments derive their just powers from the consent of the governed, and that when governments fail to accomplish the ends for which they were instituted, it is the right and duty of the people to alter and to abolish them.

It has become the custom in our time to decry

these statements as glittering generalities. They
are nothing of the kind. You may dissent from
them, you may pronounce them totally wrong,
you may assert that absolute monarchy is the true
form of government; yet these principles as laid
down in the Declaration of Independence are just
as truly the principles of government by the
people, as the divine right of kings was once the
foundation of absolute monarchy.

But the question which concerns us this afternoon is, did the fathers really believe — did they
accept the self-evident truths? Did they embody
them in the forms of government they now established? With the recommendation of May 15,
1776, every semblance of obedience to royal
authority disappeared. The people of each colony, one by one, acted on the recommendation
and in eleven of the thirteen colonies, in the course
of a few years, they formed constitutions and
governments of their own. With the teachings
of the Declaration they were perfectly familiar.
It was read in every city, town and village the
country over, and it was printed in every newspaper. No state paper of the time was so widely
circulated and so heartily endorsed. It would
seem therefore no more than reasonable to expect
that, if the men of 1776, really believed the bold
assertions it contained, their new constitutions
would be the complete embodiment of the three
great rights of man, the rights for which they
staked their lives, their fortunes and their sacred

honor. But an examination of these state constitutions reveals the fact that in their formation
very little regard was paid to the self-evident
truths, and that the very men who were loudly
asserting the political equality of man went on
and set up governments under which political
equality had no existence.

These constitutions consist, in almost every
instance, of a body of political maxims known as
the Bill or the Declaration of Rights, and an
assemblage of administrative provisions classified
as Legislative, Executive and Judicial. The
political maxims are those which a long and bitter
experience had led the people of the mother country to establish as the great principles of English
liberty (trial by jury, liberty of the press, habeas
corpus, freedom of speech, right of petition, no
excessive bail, and so on), and those which set
forth the new ideas of government which had
done so much to bring about the Revolution.

" All men," says the constitution of New
Hampshire, " are born equally free and independent; therefore, all government of right originates
from the people, is founded on the consent and
instituted for the general good. All men have
certain natural, essential and inherent rights
among which are life, liberty, the acquisition and
possession of property."

" The end of the institution, maintenance and
administration of government," says the constitution of Massachusetts, " is to secure the existence

of the body politic, to protect it and so secure to the individuals who compose it their natural rights and the blessings of life. Government is instituted for the common good, for the protection, safety, prosperity and happiness of the people, and not for the profit, honor, and private interest of any one man, family or class of men.''

" All governments ought to be instituted,'' says the constitution of Pennsylvania, " for the security and protection of the community as such, and to enable the individuals who compose it to enjoy their natural rights.''

" All governments,'' say the constitutions of Delaware and Maryland, " of right originate from the people, are founded in compact only, and instituted solely for the good of the whole; that persons entrusted with the legislative and executive powers are the trustees and servants of the public.''

" All political power,'' says the constitution of North Carolina, " is vested in and derived from the people only. No man or set of men are entitled to exclusive or separate emoluments or privileges from the community, except in consideration of great public service.''

In every instance in these early state constitutions, the state is presented as created by the people, and existing solely for the good of the individual. Its sole duty is stated to be to protect him in the full enjoyment of his natural and inalienable rights. Public officials are declared to be the trustees of the people; the right of revolution is inherent in society. In no instance is the state presented as the provider of office, the creator of monopolies.

Such being the relation of the state to the individual, what were the relations of the individual to the state? All governments, said the Declaration, derive their just powers from the consent of the governed, and this consent it was one of the political maxims of the time could only be given when the government participated directly in the election of the delegates who were to exercise the just powers of government. But to break away from the customs, usages, traditions of the past, and apply these broad doctrines in all their fullness to the present was not possible, and perhaps it was not expedient. Religious training and prejudice, the time-honored distinctions of rich and poor, learned and unlearned, still held sway and went very far towards maintaining a governing class, exceedingly democratic indeed as compared with the ruling classes of other lands, but still a class. Nowhere was voting and office holding thrown open to all men notwithstanding this natural right.

In New Hampshire the voter must be a Protestant and a taxpayer. Massachusetts required him to be possessed of a freehold estate yielding an income of three pounds a year, or to have a personal estate worth sixty pounds. In Connecticut the requirement was an annual income of

[17]

seven dollars from a freehold estate, or real estate rated on the tax list as worth $134.00. New York required a freehold estate of thirty pounds, or a house rent of forty shillings. New Jersey permitted any person, male or female, black or white, native or alien, to vote who owned real estate worth fifty pounds. In Maryland the voter must have in the county in which he wished to vote a freehold of fifty pounds, or personal property of thirty pounds. Virginia limited the franchise to such as owned twenty-five acres of land, properly planted and with a house thereon at least twelve feet square on the foundation, or such as were possessed of fifty acres of wild land or a freehold or estate interest in a lot in some of the towns established by law. North Carolina required the payment of a tax. In South Carolina the voter must be a free white man, acknowledging the being of a God and believing in a future state of reward and punishment, and must have lived one year in the state, have a freehold of fifty acres or own a town lot, or have paid a tax equal to the tax on fifty acres of land. In Georgia any mechanic, any white male inhabitant owning ten pounds of property and paying a tax, not only might but must vote under a penalty of five pounds.

In many cases these restrictions were mild and probably kept but few men from the polls permanently. But the right to vote when acquired, did not carry with it by any means the right to hold office. To be eligible to the lower house of the legislature the voter must be a Protestant and have an estate worth one hundred pounds in New Hampshire; a freehold of one hundred pounds or personal estate of two hundred pounds, and must swear that he believed in the Old and New Testament and in a divine inspiration in order to be a member of the lower house in Massachusetts. A freehold of one hundred pounds above all debts was required in New York; a belief in some Protestant creed and a personal estate was required in New Jersey; while in Delaware he must not only have the proper qualifications, but he must subscribe to this oath: " I, A. B., do profess faith in God the Father, and in Jesus Christ, and in the Holy Ghost, one God blessed evermore, and I do acknowledge the Holy Scriptures of the Old and New Testaments, to be given by divine inspiration." Maryland required each member of her assembly to own a freehold of five hundred pounds and subscribe his belief in the Christian religion. In North Carolina a member of the house of commons must be possessed and continue to be possessed in fee simple or for life, of a freehold of one hundred acres of land and profess belief in the being of God and the truth of the Protestant religion. In South Carolina a representative must own five hundred acres and ten negro slaves, or real estate worth one hundred and fifty pounds sterling clear of all debt. In Georgia he must own two hundred and fifty acres of land, or property worth two hundred and fifty pounds and be a believer in the Protestant religion, before he could be eligible to the legislature.

For membership in the upper house the qualifications were the same in kind as for membership in the lower house, but twice as great in quantity. The basis of office holding was property. The man of small means might vote, but none save well-to-do Christians could legislate, and in many states none but a rich Christian could be a governor. No Hebrew, no atheist, no Roman Catholic could be a governor of New Hampshire, nor of New Jersey, nor of South Carolina, and none but a Christian in Massachusetts, Pennsylvania, Delaware, Maryland and South Carolina. Nor were religious qualifications deemed enough. Heavy property qualifications were added, for the governor must not only be pious but rich. In one state he must own property worth one hundred pounds, in another five hundred pounds, in another five thousand pounds, and in South Carolina ten thousand pounds. It was indeed true that all governments derived their just powers from the consent of the governed; yet under these early state constitutions, none but taxpaying, property-owning men could give that consent from which government derives its just powers. It was indeed true that everywhere the utmost liberty of conscience prevailed; but the man who did not exercise that liberty of conscience in such way as to become a Christian or, in some instances a Protestant, could hold no office of profit or trust under government.

What was true of the voter and the office holder was equally true of the system of representation. In but one state did it rest on population. In New England members of the upper house were chosen in districts or counties, and were in proportion to the amount of public taxes paid in each; in New York the senators from each of the four senatorial districts were in proportion to the number of freeholders owning estates above one hundred pounds in value. In Pennsylvania and Georgia there was no senate. In Maryland the senate was chosen by an electoral college; in every other state each county was the basis of representation. For the Lower House in every state it was the number of taxable polls, or the number of duly qualified voters, or the amount of taxable property, or the county that determined the number of representatives, and in no case population. The poor man counted for nothing. He was governed, but not with his consent, by his property-owning Christian neighbors. He was one of the people, but he did not count as such in the apportionment of representation. In short, the broad doctrine that governments derived their just powers from the consent of the governed, was not accepted by the " Fathers." The most they were ready to admit was that all governments derive their just powers from the consent of the taxpayer.

While the states were thus forming and adopting their constitutions, a plan for a government for the United States was under discussion in Congress. To provide such a government as would be acceptable to thirteen independent republics, differing so widely in climate, in soil, in occupation, in everything which makes up the social and economic life of a people was no easy matter. Some were agricultural, others were commercial, a few were both. Some were great states abounding in population; some were small states. Some had their limits clearly defined; others laid claim to vast stretches of territory which extended across the continent from the Atlantic Ocean to the Mississippi River. In many cases these claims conflicted. Elements so discordant produce a conflict of interests and opinion, and sixteen months passed before the Articles of Confederation went to the states for approval. Three great questions which arose in the course of the debate:

What shall be the vote cast by each state in Congress?

How much shall each state contribute to the support of the Confederacy?

What shall be done with the western lands? concern us as bearing directly on the political ideas of the time.

In the discussion of the first question, Virginia proposed that population should be the basis of representation, and suggested that in determining all questions before Congress, Rhode Island, Delaware and Georgia should each cast one vote, and every other state one vote for every fifty thousand white inhabitants, "in order that an equality in this national assembly may be preserved as nearly as possible, and that those who are bound by measures and are to pay taxes demanded by an assembly the members of which are elected not by all the people but by those of a particular district, may have the same proportional number of votes as they would have if they were personally present." But the idea was far too radical; Virginia and Pennsylvania alone supported the motion which was lost.

Virginia now asked "that each state shall have a right to send one delegate to Congress for every 30,000 of its inhabitants, and in determining questions in Congress each delegate shall have one vote." This too was voted down, as was a third proposition that the quantum of representation for each state "shall be computed by numbers proportioned according to its contribution of money, or of taxes levied and paid into the public treasury towards the annual expenses necessary for the support of the nation." This too failed, and each state was given one vote in Congress.

But the question of representation according to population was not to be disposed of in a manner so summary. The plan as reported contained one article providing for a common treasury, to be supplied by the states in proportion to the number

of inhabitants of every age, sex and quality,
except Indians not taxed, and that the number of
inhabitants should be determined by a triennial
census. Here was a test case. Here was the
application of the revolutionary doctrine, no taxation without representation. But again the
fathers rallied and voted it down. It was then
proposed to make the share of each state proportional to the value of all property except household
goods and wearing apparel, and when this failed
a proposition was adopted declaring that the share
of each state should be in proportion to the value
of all lands within its borders granted to or sur-
veyed for any person with the value of all buildings and improvements added.

The third contest was a struggle over state
rights, and was begun by a motion by Maryland
that Congress have sole and exclusive right and
power to fix the western boundaries of such states
as claimed to extend to the South Sea. The states
with sea-to-sea charters were Massachusetts, Connecticut, Virginia, the two Carolinas and Georgia.
They voted " no," of course, and refused to consent to be stripped of their western lands. But the
question was one of state rights, and when the vote
was taken every state save Maryland voted ''no.''
It was then moved that Congress have sole and
exclusive authority to fix the western limits of such
states as claimed to the Mississippi, or South Sea,
and that the land beyond this boundary so fixed
be laid out into separate and independent states.

Again every state save Maryland voted "no."

To the delegates of the land-claiming states who thus united in voting down the resolution, the proposition of Maryland undoubtedly seemed a jealous attack on their prosperity, by attempting to strip them of their western lands and of their sovereignty by proposing that Congress should fix their boundaries. But there were in the Maryland proposition the germs of two political ideas of great moment — that of a splendid public domain held in trust by Congress for the good of all, and that of new states to be formed from this domain and admitted into the union. From this position nothing could move Maryland, nor did she yield her objections and sign the articles until New York, Connecticut and Virginia had made tenders of the western lands they claimed to own.

The terms of the cessions required that Congress should do three things—sell the land and use the money to pay the domestic debt of the confederation; cut up the territory into states; and to admit into the union on the same footing as the original states when each had a population of sixty thousand free white inhabitants. Some time must elapse before there would be sixty thousand free white inhabitants in any part of the territory, and as during this period such people as were in the West must have some kind of government, the United States found itself in the position of a mother country, and was called on to frame a plan of colonial government. In so doing Congress was perfectly free to adopt what form it pleased. No restrictions of any sort had been imposed. The great ordinance of 1787, for the government of the territory of the United States northwest of the river Ohio may therefore be considered as the complete embodiment of the most advanced ideas of government in America.

Until such time as there were five thousand free white males in the territory, which might mean a population of twenty-five or thirty thousand souls, the governed were not to be consulted. Congress was to appoint a governor, three judges and a secretary, and these men were to select from the statute of any state or states such laws or parts of laws as to them seemed proper and proclaim them to be the laws of the territory.

When at last there were five thousand free males of full age representative government was to begin. A house of representatives was to be chosen consisting of one delegate for every five hundred free males. By this house ten men were to be elected and from them Congress was to commission five to serve as a Legislative Council which with the House of Representatives constituted the Legislature. To be a voter, a man must own in fee simple fifty acres of land; to be a representative, two hundred acres; to be a member of the Council, five hundred acres. Over the Legislature the governor had almost absolute power. He could convene, prorogue and dissolve it when in his opinion it seemed expedient. His veto was final and could not be overridden; but such laws as he approved were of course subject to the veto of Congress.

Nevertheless, no little progress had been made towards the realization of the self-evident truths and the rights of man. There is still a property qualification for voters and office-holders, but there is no religious test. Representation is not according to counties, or geographical areas, or electors, or ratable polls, or the amount of taxes paid annually, but according to free males. Slavery is prohibited, and the estates of persons dying intestate are to be divided equally among the heirs, which was not the common practice of the states.

While Congress was framing the Ordinance of 1787, at New York, the Constitution of the United States was in process of making at Philadelphia. The proceedings of no body of men that ever gathered in our country to form an instrument of government are so well worthy of study. The delegates to Annapolis and later to Philadelphia were brought together in response to the demands of the business men of the country, not to form an ideal plan of government but such a practical plan as would meet the business needs of the people. It was called by the people and seven states had appointed their delegates before Congress went through the form of sanctioning the meeting. The bitter experiences of ten years made it quite clear that there must be in this country one nation or thirteen separate and independent republics. The confederation had utterly failed. For a people speaking the same language, living under the same country and under the same general government, to have among them thirteen kinds of regulations of foreign trade and commerce, thirteen kinds of regulations of interstate commerce, thirteen kinds of paper money issued by thirteen different authorities on thirteen different kinds of securities or no security at all, each legal tender, and some made so under pains and penalties — for any sensible people to expect to prosper at home or be respected abroad under such conditions was absurd. The domestic debt, the price of liberty, was still unfunded, unprovided for. The foreign debt was falling due in annual installments, which were not paid, and the interest was annually defaulted. Neither Great Britain nor Spain, whose possessions surrounded us on the north, the west and the south, and whose trade was so important, would enter into a treaty of amity and commerce. British soldiers occupied our frontier ports from Lake Superior to Lake Champlain. Spain held Alabama and Mississippi, closed the Mississippi River to American trade, and planted her guns and displayed her flag on the site of Memphis. A government capable of meeting these issues must be strong and vigorous, and on the men assembled at Philadelphia devolved the responsibility of deciding whether there should be a strong and vigorous government by the states, or a strong and vigorous government by the people. With the struggles of the advocates of each sort of government, and the compromises to which in many cases they were forced, we are not concerned. The questions for us to consider are: Did they pay heed to the inalienable rights of man, did they establish a government deriving its just powers from the consent of the governed?

At a very early stage in the proceedings it was decided that the governed should have no voice in the election of the executive. The idea of such a manner of election drew from the mover of it an apology. " I am," said James Wilson of Pennsylvania, " almost unwilling to declare the mode I wish to take place, being apprehensive that it may appear chimerical. I will say however that at least in theory, I am for an election by the people." And after he had fully stated his plan, every state save Pennsylvania voted "no." The people it was said would never be well informed as to personal character, would never give a majority of their votes to any one man, would be led by active and designing men; that it would be as unnatural to refer the choice of a proper character for chief magistrate to the people as it would be to refer a trial of colors to a blind man. The extent of the country, it was said, made it impossible for the people to have the capacity to judge of the respective pretensions of the candidates. This decision against an election by the people by no means settled the manner of choice, and twenty different ways were proposed one after another before the convention adopted the one known to the Constitution.

And now a new question arose: who shall choose the electors? Again a struggle ensued for a choice by the people, and again the old arguments against the people were urged, and eight methods were suggested before the convention in desperation threw the responsibility back on the states, and left them to decide on the methods of choosing presidential electors. At the first election, in 1789, three gave the choice to the people and eight to the legislatures. In two of them the people by their votes nominated candidates from whom the legislatures made appointments.

The great struggle for the right of the governed to express their consent was over the election of members of Congress. There were those in the convention who insisted that the number of representatives should be in proportion to population, or according to actual contribution, or to quota of contribution, or to the number of free inhabitants, or to the rule of the confederation, and that representation in the senate should be on the same basis as that in the house; and there were those who insisted on absolute equality of representation in both branches. This time the friends of government by the people stood firm and forced that compromise which made representation in the house proportionate to all free persons, including those bound to service for a term of years (the redemptioners and bond-servants), and three-fifths of the negro slaves.

Here was a great step forward. But a greater yet was taken when the convention decided that no restriction should be laid on the suffrage by the constitution, but that each state for itself should regulate the right of its citizens to vote. "The electors in each state," says the Constitution, "shall have the qualifications requisite for the electors of the most numerous branch of the state legislature." To have defined and limited the suffrage would have been to erect against the liberalizing tendencies of the day a barrier only to be removed by the difficult process of amending the Constitution.

To have established manhood suffrage would have been a blow at the state constitutions. To leave the Constitution responsive to any change in any state limitation of the suffrage, was a practical and rational solution of the problem which could only be solved in time to come.

Such in brief were the political rights of man on the 4th of March, 1789, when the Constitution of the United States went into force. But what were his social and industrial rights under the law of the land? What, above all, was the condition of that great mass of the community which earns its bread in the sweat of its brow?

All manual labor when the Revolution opened

was performed by slaves, by convict servants, by redemptioners or by freemen. The negro slave in the eye of the law was a chattel, could be bought and sold, bequeathed by will, given away, mortgaged, or seized in satisfaction of a judgment. Not a civil right of any kind was his. He could not make a contract, nor give testimony against a white man in any court, nor acquire property in any way. Whatever he found, whatever he made, whatever was given him, reverted at once to his master. To teach a slave to write was not allowed anywhere; to teach him to read was permitted in a few colonies.

One step above the slaves were the convict bond-servants, or men and women in a state of temporary involuntary servitude. These people were either political offenders or felon convicts. Those guilty of political offenses, as the Scots taken in battle in 1650, the prisoners captured at the battle of Worcester in 1651, Monmouth's men, 1685, the Scots concerned in the uprising of 1678, the Jacobins of 1716, the Scots who went out in 1745, were of course of this class of offenders; and during that period, between 1650 and 1745, as many as four thousand are known to have been sent over to this country.

The felons formed the great source of supply, and had been sent over in very considerable numbers from the earliest days of colonization. From 1650 down to the Revolution the legislation of the colonies is full of acts designed to stop the importation of such persons, robbers, murderers, forgers, counterfeiters, clippers of coin, petty thieves, house-burners, street-walkers. But in every case those acts were disallowed by the King and council, and the felons came in steadily increasing numbers. Maryland and Virginia seem to have been especially favored, as tobacco planting made a great demand for laborers. One historian of Maryland declares that up to the Revolution twenty thousand came to that colony and half of them after 1750. Another authority who has made an exhaustive study of the subject, asserts that between 1715 and 1775, ten thousand felons were exported from the Old Bailey Prison in London. After the Revolution servants of this sort ceased to be sent to America, and even to Jamaica and the Barbadoes, and in 1787, Great Britain found an outlet in her newly established penal colony at Botany Bay.

But the indentured servant and redemptioner did not cease to come when the colonies became the United States. Speaking generally, the indentured servants were men, women and even children who, unable to pay their passage, signed a contract called an indenture before leaving the old world. This indenture bound the owner or master of the ship to transport them to America, and bound the emigrant after arrival in America to serve the owner, master, or their assigns, for a certain number of years. On reaching port the owner or master, whose servants they then became, sold them for their passage to the highest bidder, or for what he could get.

The redemptioner, on the other hand, was an immigrant who signed no indenture before embarking, but agreed with the shipping merchant that after reaching America he should be given a certain time (generally a month) in which to find somebody to redeem him by paying the passage money, or freight, as it was called. Should he fail to find a redeemer within a specified time, the ship captain was at liberty to sell him to the highest bidder, in which case the redemptioner became an indentured servant and was subject to the laws governing such cases.

When a ship laden with one to three hundred such persons arrived, we will say at Philadelphia, the immigrants, arranged in a long line, were marched at once to a magistrate and forced to take an oath of allegiance to the King or, later, to the United States, and then marched back to the ship to be sold. If a purchaser was not forthcoming and they remained on shipboard until the month had passed, they were frequently sold to speculators who drove them, chained together sometimes through the country, from farm to farm, in search of a purchaser.

The contract signed, the newcomer became in the eyes of the law a slave, and in both the civil and criminal code was classed with negro slaves and Indians. None could marry without consent of the master or mistress under penalty of an addition of one year's service to the time set forth in the indenture. They were worked hard, were dressed in the cast-off clothes of their owners, and might be flogged as often as the master or mistress thought necessary. If they ran away, at least two days might be added to their time of service for each day they were absent. Father, mother and children could be sold to different buyers. Such remnants of cargoes as could not find purchasers within the time specified, were bought in lots of fifty or more by a class of speculators known as " soul drivers," who drove them through the country like so many cattle and sold them for what they would bring.

In the Middle and Southern States almost all labor, skilled and unskilled, was done by slaves, redemptioners or indentured servants. The advertisements of redemptioners mention weavers, gardeners, spinners, carpenters, smiths, wheelwrights, shoemakers, and school teachers, stonecutters, bricklayers, tailors, hatters, harness makers — men and women skilled in every sort of labor then needed in the country.

Competition of this sort made the lot of the free laborer hard indeed, but it was made harder still by the usages of the time. He worked from sunrise to sunset, earned less wages in winter than in summer, was paid at irregular intervals, and if not paid at all had no lien on the product of his labor. If he were so unfortunate as to fall into debt, though it were for but a sixpence or a penny, he might at the will of his creditor be torn from his family and cast into jail, there to remain until the debt and the prison charges were paid or he died of hunger and disease.

The state of the criminal deserves consideration, for he seems to have had no rights which anybody was bound to respect. Our forefathers, on their migration from England brought with them and planted in the new world the ideas of the treatment of crime and the criminal current in the mother country of their day. Their penal codes were not their own handiwork, but were patterned after the statutes, orders and customs of England of the seventeenth and eighteenth centuries, and are marked all through with the barbarity, cruelty and inhumanity of the time. The constitutions of six states did indeed declare that cruel and unusual punishments should not be inflicted, but a very hasty examination of the criminal codes of even these states is sufficient to show the astonishing changes which have taken place within a century in the conception of cruelty. In Massachusetts, Connecticut and Rhode Island, in 1789, ten crimes were punishable by death. In Pennsylvania, in 1718, twelve crimes on first convictions and several others on second conviction were capital offenses. In 1776 this list contained twenty crimes, and the second conviction for any crime save larceny entailed death. In Virginia and afterwards in Kentucky, to swear falsely, to destroy or conceal a will, to obtain money or goods on false pretenses, to steal a horse, or a record or writ of court, or commit robbery in the highway, were but a few of twenty-seven offenses for which a man or woman might suffer death. In New York eleven crimes were capital.

For such misdeeds as did not merit death on first conviction, the common punishments were branding, whipping, cropping the ears, standing on the pillory, sitting in the stocks, or ducking. In Maryland each county was required to have an assortment of branding irons and use them unsparingly. S L on either cheek meant seditious libeller. T on the left hand meant thief. The man with an R on the shoulder was a vagabond or rogue, with an F on the cheek a Coiner twice convicted. New Hampshire branded her burglars with the letter B — on the right for the first offense, on the left hand for a second offense, on the forehead if the crime were done on the Lord's day. Connecticut put an F on the forehead of the forger of a deed, and the letter I on the villain who sold arms to the Indians, and cut off the ears of counterfeiters. In Delaware the blasphemer was flogged, stood upon the pillory and had the letter B branded on the forehead. Virginia ordained that deceitful bakers, dishonest cooks, cheating fishermen, careless fish dressers, should lose their ears.

Publicity, in the opinion of the fathers was a great corrective and deterrent of crime. In

Pennsylvania therefore the robber and the thief, whether man or woman, after receiving at the whipping-post thirty-one lashes well laid on, was condemned to wear in plain view on the left sleeve of the outer garment, between the shoulder and the elbow, a Roman T; the letter must be four inches each way and one inch wide, must be of red, blue or yellow cloth, as the magistrate pleased, must be worn from sunrise to sunset and for a period of six months. If found without the letter the penalty for the first offense was twenty-one lashes, and for the second, thirty-nine lashes and a T branded on the forehead.

Every pauper who received any aid from any county, city or place, as also his wife and children, must wear on the sleeve of the outer garment in plain view a large P of red or blue cloth, and the first letter of the place to which he belonged.

The whipping-post and the stocks were conspicuous in every city and large town, and the ducking stool was still occasionally used. In Pennsylvania counterfeiters of the colonial money were to be flogged thirty-one lashes, stood in the pillory, and have their ears cut off. Counterfeiters of the province brands were to be stood for two hours in the pillory on a market day. Any one who raised the denomination of a bill of credit was to have thirty-one lashes, was to be put in the pillory, and have his ears cut off and nailed to the post.

That punishments of these sorts were enforced down to and well into the nineteenth century there is abundant evidence. In the *Essex Gazette* of Rhode Island in 1771, William Carlisle was convicted of passing counterfeit dollars and sentenced to stand one hour in the pillory on Little Rest Hill, and next Friday to have both ears cropped, to be branded on both cheeks with the letter R, to pay a fine of one hundred dollars and stand convicted until sentence performed. In the *Boston Post Boy* of February 1763, it is recorded that at the Superior Court held at Charlestown last week, Samuel Bacon of Bedford and Merriam Fitch, wife of Benjamin Fitch of said Bedford, were convicted of being notorious cheats and of having by fraud, craft and deceit possessed themselves of fifteen hundred Johannes, the property of a third person, were sentenced to be each of them " set in the pillory one hour with a paper on their breasts and the words "A Cheat " written in capitals thereon, to suffer three months imprisonment, and to be bound to their good behavior."

The *Boston Chronicle* of November 20, 1769, says: " We learn from Worcester that on the 8th instant one Lindsay stood in the pillory there one hour, after which he received thirty stripes at the public whipping-post and was then branded in the hand. His crime was forgery." At Salem, in 1801, one Hawkins stood on the pillory for an hour for the crime of forgery, and had his ears

cropped.   In 1803, at Boston, two criminals were
sentenced to stand one hour in the pillory for two
days, and to be imprisoned two years.

In September 1787, the Boston court sentenced
five thieves to be whipped, two set on the gallows,
and a counterfeiter on the pillory.   In 1789, eleven
were sentenced in one day to be flogged in front
of the State House.   So late as 1817, in Philadelphia, a sailor was bound to the iron rings outside
the wall of the Walnut Street Prison and flogged.
In 1822, a felon was flogged on the campus of Yale
College in the presence of the students.   In 1824,
a common scold was sentenced by a Philadelphia
court of sessions to be ducked, but the sentence
was not carried out because believed to be obso-
lete.   In 1811, the Superior Court of Georgia, at
Milledgeville, sentenced one Miss Palmer to be
ducked in the Oconee, and in 1817, in the same
state sentenced another.   Later still Judge
Cranch sentenced Mrs. Anne Royal of Washington, D. C., to be ducked in the Potomac.   She
was fined instead.

As we look back on these times and behold our
country as it was when Washington took the oath
of office for the first time, we see that very scanty
recognition seems to have been given to the
equality of men, or to their inalienable rights to
life, liberty and the pursuit of happiness.   Yet
it would be the height of injustice to accuse the
fathers of inconsistency.   To have suddenly produced such a social condition as they had in mind,

to have recklessly removed from the statute books every law, to have ruthlessly broken down every custom or usage at variance with the new principles they had announced, would have been acts of disorganization of the worst kind. But they were in no sense disorganizers or anarchists. With a steadfast belief in the truth of their principles, they waited but for a chance to apply them decently and in order, and when that chance came they were applied, and the rights of man were steadily extended.

LECTURE II

LECTURE II.

In the course of my remarks I have endeavored to pass in review the beginning of constitutional government in our country in 1775–76:

1.   The enforced assumption of authority by a body of remonstrants, and the creation of the Continental Congress.

2.   The reasons for the writing of the Declaration of Independence, and the bold assertion therein of the rights of man and the social contract theory of government.

3.   The reasons for the advice of Congress to the colonies to take up civil government of their own.

4.   The formation, in consequence of this advice, of eleven written state constitutions.

5.   The embodiment, in most of these constitutions, of the declaration of the rights of man as asserted in the Declaration of Independence.

6.   The total disregard of the principles of the declaration of the rights of man in the body of these state constitutions, first, by limiting and restricting the franchise, the right to vote, to men who could fulfill certain religious and property qualifications, then by increasing religious and property qualifications for the holding of office.

7.   The utter disregard of the people, the source of all government, by basing representa-

tion, not on numbers of people but on geographical areas, on taxpayers, qualified electors, or on
the amount of taxable property.

8. The struggle for popular representation
which took place in the conventions or meetings
which formed the Articles of Confederation, the
Ordinance of 1787, and the Constitution of the
United States, the three great charters of government which were formed between the period of
the Revolution and 1790.

9. Then we reviewed the legal status of the
great unrepresented masses, and tried to show
the utter disregard, in a legal and social point of
view, of the rights of man, and had gone down
so far as to pass in review the treatment of the
criminal and what his rights were.

Now, of course, to accuse the fathers of inconsistency in this course of action — that is, of saying one thing and doing another, would be to do
them an injustice. The declarations which they
made of the rights of man seemed, from their
point of view, to be ideals which were to be lived
up to as soon as possible, and acquired in an
orderly, systematic way. This had already been
started before the Revolution closed. We find
that while it was still raging the first steps were
taken toward the acquisition, in a broad way, of
these rights of which there has been so much
said; that during that period, between the surrender at Saratoga and the adoption of the
Constitution, five states had abolished slavery by

gradual abolition laws; that slavery had been forbidden in the western territory by the famous Sixth Article of the Ordinance, and that some reforms were even started in a social as well as in a legal way.

These of course were great steps forward, but there were greater still in the next period of ten years that closed the century. Reform was the order of the day, and in the decade which followed the adoption of the Constitution, these inalienable rights of man were still further extended. During that period New Hampshire cast away the religious test once exacted of her governor and legislators, and took off poll taxes, and put the ballot in the hands of every free male of full age. Pennsylvania abolished the test oath once required of her legislators. Delaware enfranchised every free male twenty-one years old, and ceased to ask of her office-holders if they believed in the trinity and the divine inspiration of the Scriptures. South Carolina removed the religious qualification from voters, ceased to require all members of the House of Representatives to be Protestant, and greatly reduced the property qualifications for officeholding. Georgia removed the religious test for civil office, and the property qualifications for voters, gave the ballot to all free white citizens who had paid a tax, made population the basis of representation, and defined population as all white persons and three-fifths of the persons of color. The constitution of Vermont provided for manhood suffrage; and required no property qualifications for officeholding. Kentucky gave the ballot to every free white male, and had neither property nor religious qualifications for office-holders. Tennessee, of the new states, alone remained unresponsive to the spirit of the age. Her office-holders were required to own property, to believe in the existence of God and a future state of rewards and punishments, and her voters must also own a freehold. Of all the states west of the mountains, she was the only one that adopted in all their rigor the old restrictions on the subject. In general it may be said that Church and State were separated, that property qualifications were beginning to be reduced, and that the new democratic doctrine of manhood suffrage was gaining ground.

In the constitution of Pennsylvania were these words: "The penal laws as heretofore used shall be reformed by the legislature of the state as soon as may be, and punishments made in some cases less sanguinary and in general more proportionate to the crimes." While the war raged this injunction went unheeded, but by the law of 1787, three offenses theretofore punishable with death, were made punishable by the forfeiture of the real and personal estate of the offender and confinement at hard labor; all barbarous punishments were abolished, and the streets of Philadelphia ceased to be swept by men chained to wheelbarrows or dragging logs chained to their ankles.

In 1794, the death penalty was abolished save as a punishment for murder in the first degree, and in 1795, flogging was abolished and confinement in a cell with bread and water diet substituted. The rights even of criminals to life and liberty were gaining recognition. Connecticut in 1791, abolished cropping and branding, and provided that burglary, arson, forgery and horse stealing should no longer be punishable with death. In 1788, New York abolished the old medieval plea of "benefit of clergy," and in 1796, abolished capital punishment for fourteen crimes and limited it to murder and treason. Whipping for minor crimes was abolished at the same time.

Quite as remarkable was the reform in the treatment of criminals. If the descriptions of the jails and prisons of the eighteenth century are but partially true, they must have exceeded in horror the dungeons of medieval Europe. At Simsbury, Connecticut, was the Newgate prison, in an old worked-out copper mine on the hills. The entrance was down a shaft by a ladder to the caverns. In these were the cells in which were often confined from thirty to one hundred convicts, who each night were chained by the feet to the floor and by their necks to the wall. The foulness of this den surpasses description. At Northampton, Massachusetts, was a dungeon four feet high without windows. At Worcester was another such dungeon, said to be but three feet high. The old Market Street Prison in Philadelphia was presented by the Grand Jury in 1787, as a nuisance. Men and women of all ages were thrust into one large compartment, and with them were confined others held as witnesses or guilty of no greater offense than an honest inability to pay their debts.

No records of the past furnish more horrible reading than those in which are told the horrors of the debtors' prisons. For the smallest debt possible, though it were but a cent, the body of the debtor, whether man or woman, could be seized by the creditor and cast into jail, there to remain till the sum was paid in full. By an old law which went back to the days when Pennsylvania was a colony, magistrates were allowed cognizance without appeal of debts under forty shillings, or $5.33. When the debt exceeded that sum the debtor was entitled to a stay of execution. But no such privilege was accorded the wretch who owed a sixpence or a shilling, and who might if his creditor chose, be dragged to jail on what were truly called " spite actions.'' Once behind the bars his lot was harder than that of the lowest criminals. Thieves and counterfeiters, murderers and felons of every sort were fed and cared for at the expense of the state, but for the luckless debtor no such provision was made. The food he ate, the clothes that covered him, were provided, if provided at all, by his friends or by the charity of the public or by some Society for Alleviating the Misery of Public Prisons. The

room in which he was confined with scores of
hardened offenders was utterly without furniture
of any sort. In it were neither chairs, tables,
cots, nor so much as a bench. He sat on the
floor, ate off the floor, and at night lay down to
sleep on the floor without a blanket to cover him.
Against this violation of the rights of man to
liberty, society at last rebelled, and in 1794, a
change for the better was ordered. "Whereas,"
said the law, "many persons confined in the
prison called the debtors' apartment in the city
of Philadelphia are so poor as to be unable to
procure food for their sustenance, or fuel, or
clothing in the winter season, and it is inconsistent with humanity to suffer them to want the
common necessaries of life, the state must " — we
might suppose the law would say " abolish imprisonment for debt under forty shillings," — but
the law said nothing of the kind — the state must
order the inspector to provide fuel and blankets
for such debtors as by reason of their poverty
could not get them, and should allow each debtor
seven cents a day for food! For twenty years the
community seems to have thought this was all
humanity required, and no further change was
made in the condition of the debtors' prison until
1814.

At the opening of the nineteenth century, therefore, the political rights of man had been materi-
ally advanced, the abolition of slavery was well
under way, the Northwest Territory had been

dedicated to freedom, cruel and barbarous forms of punishment were beginning to disappear, and some reforms in the treatment of criminals and debtors had just been started.

The first decade of the new century was preeminently a period of attempted social rather than of political reform. The decade opened with the triumph of democracy. The election of Mr. Jefferson was in no sense a mere political victory at the polls, the success of one party over another. It marks an epoch in our history. It was the placing in power of a party which from its very origin in 1792, was the pronounced advocate of the rights of man and the doctrines of the Declaration of Independence. In the opinion of every follower of Jefferson, every follower of Washington was a monarchist and aristocrat. The attempt to give the president a title, the secret sessions of the senate, the gowns of the judges, the exclusive levees of the president, and the coach with outriders; the annual speech to Congress, in imitation of the king's speech from the throne; the ball on the president's birthnight — were all of them sure signs of a leaning towards aristocracy. The funding system, the great national debt, the national bank, were monarchical institutions which stamped the ideas of the party responsible for them.

On the other hand, every follower of Jefferson, in the eyes of the Federalists was a Jacobin, a leveller, a socialist. We should expect that when this much reviled party came to power a great movement of democracy would take place, that all the evils which were portrayed by the Federalist party would fall upon the country, and that the rights of man would be very greatly extended. But nothing of the sort occurred. Indeed, the party of the rights of man had not been many months in power when Louisiana was purchased, and they were called on to frame a government for the Territory of Orleans. And what sort of government was given to the Territory of Orleans? The president was authorized to appoint annually without consulting the senate in any way, thirteen discreet landowners to form a council. This council met when the governor summoned it, and went home when he dismissed it. It could not frame a law but could merely criticize such laws as the governor would please to lay before it. Not an official of any sort was elected, not a vote was given. The consent of the governed, from which all governments derive their just powers, was not even asked. Yet this bill which established this government was signed by the man who wrote the Declaration of Independence.

Yet there was some progress made in the political rights of man elsewhere. New Jersey did away with her property qualification for voters, and established manhood suffrage by the simple process of declaring that her constitution did not mean what it said. Maryland, too, adopted manhood suffrage. Ohio gave the ballot to all white

[53]

male inhabitants of full age who paid a tax, and made representation proportional to the number of white male inhabitants above the age of twenty-one.

The great feature of the decade, however, was the struggle for industrial rights. From such statistics of the pay of unskilled labor in 1800, as can now be gathered, it appears that wages differed in the three great belts along which population was moving westward. The highest rates were paid in the New England belt, which stretched across the country from Massachusetts to Ohio. The lowest rates prevailed in the southern belt, which extended from the Carolinas to Louisiana. In each of these bands, again, wages were lowest on the Atlantic seaboard and, increasing rapidly in a western direction, were greatest in the Mississippi valley. They varied again with the sex of the laborer, for men were paid most and women least. They rose and fell with the seasons of the year, for there was one rate for winter when the days were short, and another for summer when the days were long, and a third for harvest time when work was plenty and the laborers few. And they varied with the conditions of labor, being greatest when the workman fed and lodged himself, and lowest when he was fed, lodged and provided with grog by his employers.

Thus, in the district of Maine, at Haverhill and about Boston, laborers when fed, were paid seven dollars per month in winter and ten in summer.

Passing westward the scale rose, and at Springfield men were paid nine dollars, at Stonington ten dollars, at Stockbridge twelve, at Catskill thirteen, at Hudson fourteen per month, provided in each case they fed themselves. In the Genesee country and along the Lakes hiring by the month was not common, and there the unskilled workman was paid one dollar a day for laboring from sunrise to sunset. Throughout Central Pennsylvania eight dollars per month of twenty-six working days was paid to farm hands, when fed and lodged. Boatmen on the Ohio received one dollar per day. In the southern belt the negro was the chief laborer and when he was hired out, as was the case in all the towns, his owner was paid eighty dollars per year. On the Mississippi the boat hands were fed and paid one dollar per working day.

Between 1800 and 1810, the spread of population, the increase in the number of firms, the rush of men into the merchant marine, raised the pay of the unskilled laborer very perceptibly. From the estimates of the cost of internal improvements, from the pay-rolls of turnpike companies, from town records, from private diaries, from newspaper advertisements, it appears that during this period men who could drive piles, or build roads, or dig ditches, or pave streets, or tend a machine in any of the factories, or were engaged in transportation, were paid from a dollar to a dollar and a third per day. One advertise-

ment for thirty men to work on the road from
Genesee River to Buffalo offers twelve dollars
a month, food, lodging and whiskey every
day.

The wages of skilled workmen, however, under-
went no such increase. A few classes of artisans
greatly in demand, as ship-carpenters, were paid
two dollars per day. But they were the exception, and such trades as had labor organizations
now attempted to force up wages by strikes.
Labor organizations for benevolent purposes
solely, were characteristic of the opening years of
the century, and indeed nothing is more characteristic of the opening years of the nineteenth
century than the rapidity with which benevolent
societies of all sorts came into existence. Such
as were purely labor organizations were, in general, of two sorts: societies composed of men of
one craft living in one city, and societies made
up of artisans following these trades. Associations of journeymen of one craft were, at first,
for benevolent and charitable purposes only.
But in the flush times of 1800 to 1810, they became
agitators for the rights of labor. Thus in 1800,
the Federal and Union Society of Journeymen
Tailors in Philadelphia in a long address to the
public, complain of the low wages they are paid,
of the unjust conduct of their employers, who
give out work to women and indifferent trades-
men, who are glad to work for the lowest wages.
They declare that they will not serve such

masters and give the names of nine offending employers.

Four years later the journeymen tailors in Baltimore who were receiving seven shillings and sixpence for making a coat or a waistcoat, or a pair of knee-breeches, went on strike and forced up their pay to eight shillings and ninepence per job; and secured such a system of extras that what had been four jobs counted as eight. Almost at the same time the journeymen cordwainers of Philadelphia struck against a rate of wages which made it impossible by working from sunrise to sunset to earn more than eleven dollars per week. But the strike of that year was stoutly resisted, and the strikers brought to trial in the mayor's court, charged with conspiracy to raise their wages. Just at that moment the *Aurora* was engaged in an attack on the English common law, which a judge had declared to be in force in Pennsylvania, and as the indictment had been obtained under the common law, Duane made the cause of the shoemakers his own. Among the blessings promised mankind by the Revolution was, he said, the emancipation of industry from the fetters forged by luxury, laziness, aristocracy and fraud. Hitherto the people had traveled the level road to equal justice. No monopoly had been tolerated save patent rights. Of all the barbarous principles of feudalism entailed on us by England, none was left but slavery, and even this would be greatly restricted in 1808. Yet would it be believed at the very time when the state of the negro was about to be improved, attempts were being made to reduce the whites to slavery. Was there anything in the Constitution of the United States or in the Constitution of Pennsylvania, which gave one man a right to say to another what should be the price of his labor? There was not. It was by the English common law that such things became possible. When the trial was over and the men found guilty of a combination to raise their wages, the defeated journeymen appealed for help to a sympathetic public. "The journeymen cordwainers of Philadelphia," so runs their appeal, "respectfully inform the inhabitants that they have opened a Boot & Shoe Warehouse at 44 S. Third Street. The unprecedented trial which issued in their conviction, as well as the unfortunate circumstances in which they find themselves after so long a contest, are the reasons which induce them to make trial of the public liberality to save themselves and their families from abject poverty."

A few years later, in 1808, the journeymen tailors a second time struck at Baltimore. Each side appealed to the impartial public. The journeymen demanded ten shillings per job or nine dollars per week, which was no more, they said, than was paid to the common laborer, who had not spent an hour in learning his business, while they had spent an apprenticeship of seven years in learning theirs. The master tailors answered that the journeymen were becoming high-handed. Not only had they refused to work at the old wages, but they had forced men who were willing to work to stop, and had threatened to tar and feather any lawyer who prosecuted them. Few masters in the city made a thousand suits a year, and none were paid more than seven dollars for making one. To yield to the demand of the journeymen was therefore impossible; unless gentlemen were willing to pay more for their clothes. The end was a compromise.

From Baltimore discontent spread to New York, and in October 1809, the cordwainers of that city went out on strike. The society was well organized, had on its rolls about one hundred and eighty-six members, and seems to have been careful to enforce its rules, some of which were most tyrannical. Every journeyman coming to the city must join the society, or a strike against the shop where he was employed would follow. When he did join the shop he ceased, so far as his trade was concerned, to be a freeman. He could not agree with his employer as to the wages for which he would work. He could not remain in a shop if the master cordwainer employed an apprentice who was not a member of the society, or employed more than two apprentices who were members of the society. If a member broke any of the rules a demand was made on his employer for his discharge, and if not complied with a strike was ordered against the shop. Strikes of this kind seem to have been common. One happened in 1809, but the firm sent their work to other shops. The journeymen found it out, and a general strike was ordered. The masters followed the example set in Philadelphia — the strikers were arrested and tried for conspiracy to raise their wages. The case came on in the mayor's court in 1809. DeWitt Clinton was then mayor. His term was nearly ended, and not wishing to antagonize either party, he twice postponed decision. In April, 1810, Jacob Radcliff succeeded him, and not having heard the argument made before Clinton, put off the case to a special session in July 1810. The journeymen were then found guilty, admonished by the mayor, and fined one dollar each with costs — which the mayor promptly paid!

Next came the cordwainers of Albany, eighty in number. They too demanded an increase of wages, and when it was refused went out on strike. Thereupon the master cordwainers inserted in the Boston, Hartford, New York and Philadelphia newspapers an advertisement offering employment to two hundred and fifty journeymen. But the Albany strikers inserted in the same paper a card headed " Caution," in which they declared that two hundred and fifty men were not needed in Albany; that the purpose of the masters was to bring a great crowd of applicants to the city, select the best of the lot and force them, through fear of competition and of being left in a strange city without employment, to accept a mere pittance as wages.

The second decade of the century was pre-eminently a period of constitution making. During it seven states entered the Union, and one of the old states, Kentucky, made her first constitution. The hard times on the seaboard, the commercial and industrial depression which followed the close of the second war with Great Britain, sent a wave of population over the mountains to the Mississippi Valley, and built up, in the short period of five years, the states of Indiana, Illinois, Alabama, Mississippi and Missouri. A sixth, Louisiana, was the direct result of the Louisiana purchase. A seventh, Maine, had heretofore been part of Massachusetts. In every one of these states the rights of man were broadly recognized in their constitutions. Four gave the ballot to white males. Two restricted the franchise to free white males who paid a tax. Two based representation in the lower branch of the legislature on white population, three on white males, two on the voting population. The old idea that taxation should be the basis of representation was rapidly giving way to the new one. That all men should vote, that the people should be represented, and not freehold estates, or personal property, or political areas or counties or towns, were now fast becoming self-evident truths. Some of the new states made truth a good defense in libel suits. Some provided that the estates of suicides should be divided equally among the heirs, just as in the case of natural death. By an old law of New Jersey, the estates of intestates were to be so divided that each male should receive twice as much as each female heir. But the day of equal rights had dawned and yielding to the spirit of the times, New Jersey repealed her old law and in a new one ordained that the estates of persons who left no will should be divided equally among the heirs. Other states abolished imprisonment for small debts.

The last half of the decade was especially favorable to the extension of the rights of man, for never had the suffering of the weaker, poorer and dependent part of the community attracted so much attention. The hard times caused by the second war with Great Britain were made harder yet by the ruin of trade, commerce and agriculture which followed the downfall of Napoleon and the peace. The splendid carrying trade between the powers of Europe and their new world colonies was gone. The fine market for the food products of the United States, built up by two and twenty years of almost continuous warfare, was gone. Our vessels were shut out of the British West Indies. The currency was in disorder. British competition had all but ruined manufactures, and our country entered on four years of the worst times it has ever known. The boldest and most enterprising of the sufferers fled from the seaboard states to the Mississippi Valley, where government land could be bought for two dollars an acre and paid for in installments; and where the purchaser was exempt for five years from state taxation; but the weaker remained to swell the poorhouses, the debtors' prisons and the jails.

From documents presented to the Senate of New York in 1817, it appeared that the keeper of the debtors' prison in New York City certified that, during 1816, 1,984 debtors were confined, and that upwards of 600 were always in the jail or on its limits. The sheriff of the county certified that 1,129 were in prison for debts under fifty dollars, that of these 729 owed less than twenty-five dollars each, and that every one of them would have starved to death but for the kindness of the Humane Society. Indeed, he had more than once been forced to buy fuel with his own money to keep them from freezing. One man who had been confined for a debt of fifty dollars had remained in jail three years, and during this entire time had been fed and clothed by the Humane Society. Another debtor had been imprisoned for six years and supported by charity. A typical case occurred in Vermont which illustrates the gross injustice of the system. The debtor owed a firm of two, fifty-four cents. The two members of the firm divided the debt, and each had the debtor imprisoned for twenty-seven cents. The costs in each action were: Execution, $1.75; officer's fees, $2.18; jailor's fees, 50 cents;

citation, 34 cents; service, $1.25; commissioner's fees, $1.25. Total, $7.27. The total costs in both cases were $14.54. If the poor man could not pay the original debt of 54 cents it was idle to expect him to pay $14.54 costs in addition. But revenge is sweet and to jail he went.

In the face of such evidence, the legislature of New York relented, and in 1817, forbade the imprisonment of debtors for sums less than $25.00. This led the way and state after state followed. In 1818, New Hampshire exempted her inhabitants from arrest for debts under $13.33. A year later Vermont abolished imprisonment for debts under $15.00. Pennsylvania and Kentucky were not willing to go so far, yet each amended her law and forbade the imprisonment of women for debts of any amount.

In states where public opinion was indifferent, the horrors of the debtors' prison continued to grow worse and worse. A Report of the Society for the Relief of the Distressed, published in Boston, sets forth that between January 1820, and April 1822, 3,492 persons were imprisoned for debt in Boston; that 2,000 were deprived of their liberty for sums less than $20.00; that 430 of these were women, and that the suffering caused to the families of those in prison affected more than 10,000 human beings. The agents of the society found a woman in the prison who owed $3.60, and for this sum had been dragged from her home and two children under three years of age. One debtor had been confined thirty years, and when the society brought his case to light his friends had utterly forgotten him. But they came nobly to his aid, and raised the $3,000 necessary to pay the jail fees and costs that had accumulated during the long period of imprisonment.

The Report of the Boston Prison Discipline Society for 1828, cites the case of a mechanic sent to jail for a debt of $5.00 contracted at the grocer's while he lay ill with a fever. The keeper of the debtor's prison in Philadelphia reported in 1828, that during the year 1,085 persons had been confined; that the sum total of their debts was $25,409; that the amount recovered from prisoners by creditors was $295.00, and that the cost to the community for maintaining the prison and the debtors was $285,000. The next year, 1829, thirty-two persons were in jail in Philadelphia for debts under one dollar, and in the thirty prisons of the state were 595 persons owing debts of from one to five dollars. In 1831 there were in Philadelphia forty debtors imprisoned for the gross sum of twenty-three dollars. One man owed two cents, another seventy-two cents. Seven were confined 172 days for $2.84, and the only debt recovered during fifteen months was one for seventy-five cents. In the Arch Street Prison 100 debtors per month were received. No attendance nor medicine were provided for the sick, no beds, no clothing were supplied them. "A bed," says the report, "is seldom seen in this prison. No provision is made by law for either sex, though some 4,500 are sent here annually. It is a common receptacle for all untried prisoners. Robbers, vagrants, petty thieves, burglars are here confined with debtors and witnesses. In New Jersey food, bedding and fuel were provided for criminals, but for debtors only walls, bars and bolts. Many of the debts are described as ' rum debts '; they had been incurred at the grog-shops and corner groceries.

Bad as all this was, the condition of the debtor was steadily improving. If it was true that man was entitled to life, liberty and the pursuit of happiness as three of his inalienable rights, then liberty was not to be restrained nor the pursuit of happiness prevented, save in punishment of crimes of the most serious nature. Admitting this to be true, imprisonment for debt save where fraud was shown or suspected, was abolished in Kentucky in 1821, in Ohio in 1828, in New Jersey and Vermont in 1830, in Maryland, for debts less than thirty dollars, in 1830. Massachusetts, in 1831, exempted all males from imprisonment for debts under ten dollars, and females for debts of any amount. New York, after a long and bitter contest fought out in the press and in the legislature, abolished imprisonment for debt in 1832. Connecticut followed in 1837, Louisiana in 1840, Missouri in 1845, and Alabama in 1848.

Meantime the political and industrial rights of

man were being greatly extended, even in the old and conservative states. Under the constitution of New York, framed in 1777, the males were arranged in three great classes: those who could not cast a vote for any state officer, the twenty-pound freeholders and forty-shilling renters who could vote for members of Assembly, and the one-hundred-pound freeholders who were electors of assemblymen, senators and lieutenant-governor and governor. But the narrow interpretation which the law placed on the word "freeholder" deprived of a vote many a man entitled to it. In the eye of the law a man who possessed a piece of real estate worth £20 or £100, that is, $50.00 or $250.00, was entitled to the franchise. But a man who held an estate in a farm or city lot for nine hundred and ninety-nine years, was a lease-holder and could not vote, though the land was worth thousands of dollars. In this class were thousands of farmers who as lessees of the great Dutch manors held their land for nine hundred and ninety-nine years. A second class of disfranchised landholders were the men who had purchased their farms on the installment plan from the Holland Land Company or the Pultney and Hornby estates. In place of selling in fee simple and taking back a mortgage, these great land-owners would sell on long credit with payments at certain intervals, and execute a contract to convey by deed when the last installment had been paid. Were or were not these "equitable freeholders,'' as they were called, true freeholders within the meaning of the law and entitled to vote ? The common belief was that they were not, and they cast no votes. Nevertheless, a statute had been enacted which permitted them to act as jurors. But a juror must be a freeholder, and the question of the status of the equitable freeholder became more complicated than ever. In other parts of the state it was a common custom to give a deed and take back a mortgage as security for payment. Who owned such a piece of land, the mortgagor or the mortgagee? With which did the freehold rest? The law said with both, and gave a vote to the man who happened to be in actual possession.

The doubt cast on the meaning of '' freeholder '' by these statutes, the disfranchisement of fifty thousand taxpaying farmers, and the steadily growing belief that manhood suffrage was the true principle of democratic government made this state of affairs unendurable, and in 1821, a convention to amend the constitution gathered at Albany. That the old property qualification for electors of governor and assembly should be abolished was generally conceded. But a strong minority insisted that in the senate property should be represented and that no man should vote for a senator who did not have in his own or his wife's right an interest, in law or in equity, in lands or tenements in the state to the value of two hundred and fifty dollars. Government, it was argued, is founded for the protection of life, liberty and property. Each, therefore, ought to be represented so as to ensure its protection. It was the opinion of our ancestors that there should be two branches in the legislative department, to be mutual checks upon each other. But the amendment offered to this convention is calculated utterly to do away with that safeguard which these checks had raised. If the members of the senate are elected by the same persons, possessed of the same sentiments, views and passions, and the same interests and objects as those who elect the popular branch, it will result that although they meet in separate chambers, they will be governed by the same feelings and will cease to be the least possible check on the other branch of the legislature.

Should this amendment succeed, it was further argued, not only the same class will elect, but that class will be extended, and then where will be the security of the landed interests of the state? Suppose a legislature thus elected should think fit to levy all the taxes and impose all the burdens of the government upon the landed interests only, what power could prevent them? " Sir," said the speaker, " we are legislating for posterity and our votes should have reference to the permanence of the government. I will go as far as any man to extend the right of suffrage, when there is a probable prospect that it will be exercised in a pure and independent manner. Is not property desirable? Is it not worth protecting? All that goes to embellish or render society valuable depends upon it. Churches and hospitals are erected and schools established by property, and every government that has the interests and prosperity of the governed at heart must feel bound to protect it.''

'' I am not,'' said Chancellor Kent, '' prepared to annihilate all distinction and cause all to bow before the right of universal suffrage. This democratic principle cannot be contemplated without terror. We have seen its career in Europe, and their experience should be to us a voice of warning. It would be madness to expect exemption from those passions by which other nations have been first inflamed and then destroyed. The senate is the sheet-anchor of the people's safety, and without it the agricultural interest is committed to the winds. In the hands of moderate and small farmers liberty is not likely to be lost. In that body will be found honesty, independence, temperance and justice. They are the surest guardians of property, and they constitute the firmest basis of national power.

'' It is to protect this important class that the senate should be preserved. It should be the representative of property, of landed interests, and its security against the caprice of the motley crowd of paupers, emigrants, journeymen manufacturers, and those undefined classes of inhabitants a state and city like ours is calculated to invite. Universal suffrage jeopardizes property and puts it into the power of the poor and the profligate to control the affluent. Shall every department of the government be at the disposal of those who are often ignorant of the importance and nature of the right they are authorized to assume? The poor man's interest is always in opposition to his duty, and it is too much to expect of human nature that interest will not be consulted. And surely that class and description of persons having the power in one branch of the legislature to forbid the passage of a law they think injurious to their personal right, are safe and have no reason to complain.'' In the end it was decided that senators must be freeholders.

The same contest raged over the question of suffrage. The committee which reported to the convention abolished all existing distinctions, and proposed to give the ballot to every white man who paid a tax in money or in service, who worked one day per annum on the high roads, or served in the militia. But this was not going far enough, and demands were at once made for the inclusion of the black men.

That all men are born free and equal, it was said, is a maxim true only in a state of nature. In society this general equality is restrained for the public good. On this principle the blacks are excluded. They are required to bear no burdens, perform no duties. The blacks are a peculiar people, unacquainted with civil liberty and incapable of appreciating its benefits. We exclude aliens, we exclude minors, we exclude the better part of creation — woman — and no complaints are made. Yet these are all "born free and equal." It was idle to cite the Declaration of Independence to prove that the blacks are possessed of certain inalienable rights. The right of voting is not a natural right. A natural right is one born with us. No man is born twenty-one years old, therefore all restraint put on the right of voting during the period of nonage is usurpation and tyranny. This confusion arises from mixing natural and acquired rights. The right of voting is resorted to merely as a means of securing our natural rights. Your law says that jurors shall be freeholders. Was a negro freeholder ever put on a jury? If so, no white man would sit with him. Yet gentlemen who would shrink from such association now proposed to associate with him in the important duty of electing a governor and assembly. If you admit the negro, why exclude women and Indians? They have never been enslaved; they are born free as the air they breathe. We ought to make a constitution suited to our habits, customs and usages. Metaphysical refinements are of no use in framing a constitution. No white man will stand shoulder to shoulder with a negro in the train-band or the jury room, or invite him to his table or into his pew in church. Why then put him on an equality on election day?

These arguments were partially successful, and while the ballot was given to every white male citizen who had lived one year in the state and paid a tax or served in the militia, or having lived three years in the state had been assessed to labor on the highways, and had performed that labor or paid the equivalent in money, no negro could vote unless he had lived three years in the state, and owned a freehold worth two hundred and fifty dollars and had paid a tax thereon. In the opinion of Martin Van Buren who was a member of this convention, this extension of suffrage for whites was carried too far. It was practically universal suffrage. He was disposed to go as far as any man in the extension of rational liberty, but he could not consent to undervalue this precious privilege so far as to confer it indiscriminately on every one, black and white, who would be kind enough to condescend to accept it.

In Massachusetts a like contest had just taken place. Even in that conservative state the spirit of the age was at work, and the old constitution of 1780, had become, by 1820, so antiquated that a convention was called to revise, amend and modernize it. The great question which the reformers had to answer was, will the rights of property be respected in a state where every man may cast a vote? Is it not a fundamental principle of our system of government, that if representation in one branch of the legislature is based on population, the other should be based on property? How else can you maintain the checks and balances? If you have the right to disfranchise the pauper, the man without one dollar, haven't you the same right to disfranchise the man not worth two hundred and fifty dollars? If suffrage is one of the natural rights of man, then you could not disfranchise a pauper.

But the answer to these questions and the contest which followed them is a subject too long to be taken up this afternoon. I will begin with it, therefore, with your permission, tomorrow.

LECTURE III

LECTURE III.

We left the subject at a point where the people of Massachusetts were about to make their second constitution. The ideas of the rights of man had been so generally accepted at that time that there was no question as to whether there should be a religious or property qualification for a voter or for minor office-holders, or for members of the lower house of the general court. But the contest for the rights of property as against the rights of man was waged over the question of qualifications for membership in the senate and for voting in the senate. The plan before the convention was that a property qualification should be required for the persons who wished to vote for a senator or wished to be eligible to the senate, the qualification being the same as in the old constitution, the ownership of two hundred dollars' worth of property.

That matter had just been fought out in the constitutional convention in New York, and had resulted in a general franchise for all voters and office-holders except negroes, who were required to have a freehold of two hundred and fifty dollars.

The argument made in the convention in Massachusetts was to the effect, that if you can forbid a man who has no money — a pauper — to vote,

you may at the same time, with the same right,
disfranchise the man who has not two hundred
and fifty dollars; that if suffrage is one of the
natural rights — an inalienable right of man —
then you cannot exclude either paupers or persons
under twenty-one years of age. But, in truth,
there is no question of right, it is entirely a question of expediency. It is expedient to retain the
qualification in the constitution. It is in the
nature of a privilege and, as such, is connected
with many virtues which conduce to the good
order of society. It is a distinction to be sought
for, and is the reward of good conduct. It
encourages industry, economy and prudence; it
elevates the standard of all our civil institutions;
and gives dignity and importance to those who
choose and those who are chosen. It acts as a
stimulus to exertion to acquire what it is a distinction to possess. The speaker maintained that
in this country, where the means of subsistence
were so abundant, and the demand for labor so
great, every man of sound body could acquire the
necessary qualification. If he failed to do this it
must be, ordinarily, because he was indolent or
vicious. In many of the states a qualification of
freehold was required. He thought that a wise
provision, and if any alteration was to be made
he should be in favor of placing it there rather
than upon personal property. As it was, he
thought it valuable as a moral means, as part of
that moral force so essential to the support of any

free government. He considered it as unreasonable, that a man who had no property should act indirectly upon the property of others. If gentlemen would look to the statute book, to the business of the legislature, or to the courts of law, how much of all that was done would be found to relate to the rights of property. It lay at the foundation of the social state, it was the spring of all action and all employment. It was therefore, he apprehended, wholly inequitable in its nature that men without a dollar should in any way determine the rights of property or have any concern in its appropriation. He also contended that the principle of the resolution was antirepublican. It greatly increased the number of voters, and those of a character most liable to be improperly influenced or corrupted. It enlarged the field of action to every popular favorite, and enabled him to combine greater numbers. The time might come when he would be able to command, as truly as ever a general commanded an army, sufficient numbers to affect or control the government itself. In that case the form of a republican constitution might remain but its life and spirit would have fled. The government would be essentially a democracy, and between that and a despotism there would be but one step. Such would be the tendency of the principle, and so far as it operated it would change the structure of the constitution. The qualification which it required was intended as a security for property. He considered it as a barrier which ought not to be removed, and could not be without danger to the state.

The assertion has been made, said another speaker, that no fundamental principle of the government was to be changed. This proposition did change a fundamental principle. It was not the admission or the rejection of a few votes in the existing state of things. But it was a change which might, at some time or other, produce a result widely different from what gentlemen apprehended. It went directly to sap the foundations of society. He asked if there were too many incentives to industry and economy at present? Apprentices and the sons of poor farmers were induced to lead a life of industry and economy, that when they arrived at the age provided by law they might be prepared to exercise the rights of freemen. This alone was sufficient to determine his vote. But there were other considerations It was an anti-republican principle. He proceeded to state in what manner a rich man in a populous town might command the votes of men without any property, and consequently destitute of character. It now very seldom happened that a man of industrious habits and regular life was excluded from the right of voting. Even men of character who through misfortune are obliged to call on towns for aid, often have property enough to entitle them to vote. The household furniture, exempted by law from attachment, is nearly enough to give them the right. Very few but vagabonds are excluded.

Another member of the convention said he recollected that in 1775, the saying was current that taxation and representation should go hand in hand. Take this text and apply it to the men who are excluded by this qualification from the right of voting. Who are they? The laboring parts of society. How long have they been fettered? Forty years. Who achieved our independence? This class of men. And shall we then disfranchise them? I hope not. As the constitution now is these men are deprived of voting and must stand by and see the rich putting in their votes. Though a man was a Newton or a Locke, if he is poor he may stand by and see his liberties voted away. Suppose an invasion should happen — these men would be obliged to come forward in defense of their country. He felt conscientiously bound to give them the right of voting.

Gentlemen, said yet another member, who were unwilling to change the principles of the constitution, instead of striking out this qualification ought to increase the sum on account of the change in the value of money. He thought, however, that it would be impossible for them to effect this change without a radical departure from the fundamental principles of good government. He would not contend against the right of requiring it, though there were strong arguments on that side, but he considered it inexpedient to make the change. The provision could not be carried into effect; it was the cause of perjury and immorality; it did not prevent a fraudulent man, who owed more than he was worth, from voting but debarred an honest man who paid his debts; and it tended to throw suspicion of unfairness on the municipal authority.

Of all the arguments made against universal suffrage the best known in our day is that made by Daniel Webster, for a few days after he made it before the convention he embodied it word for word in the famous Plymouth Oration. " If," said Webster, " the two houses are to be chosen in the manner proposed, there is obviously no other check or control than a division into separate chambers. The members of both houses are to be chosen at the same time, by the same electors, in the same districts, and for the same term of office. They will of course all be actuated by the same feelings and interests. Whatever motives may at the moment exist to elect particular members of one house, will operate equally on the choice of members for the other. There is so little of real utility in this mode that, if nothing more be done, it would be more expedient to choose all the members of the legislature without distinction, simply as members of the legislature, and to make the division into two houses, either by lot or otherwise, after these members, the chosen should have come up to the capital.

" I wish now, sir, to correct a most important mistake in the manner in which this question has been stated. It has been said that we propose to give property, merely as such, a control over the people numerically considered. But this I take to be not at all the true nature of the proposition. The senate is not to be a check on the *people* but on the *House of Representatives.* It is the case of an authority given to *one* agent to check or control the acts of *another.* The people having conferred on the House of Representatives powers which are great and from their nature liable to abuse, require for their own security another house which shall possess an effectual negative on the first. This does not limit the power of the people, but only the authority of their agents. It is not a restraint on their rights, but a restraint on the power that they have delegated. It limits the authority of agents in making laws to bind their principals. And if it be wise to give one agent the power of checking or controlling another it is equally wise, most manifestly, that there should be some difference of character, sentiment, feeling or origin in that agent who is to possess this control. Otherwise it is not at all probable that the control will ever be exercised. To require the consent of two agents to the validity of an act, and yet to appoint agents so similar in all respects as to create a moral certainty that what one does the other will do, also would be inconsistent and nugatory.

There can be no effectual control without some difference.

" The true principle of a free and popular government would seem to be so to construct it as to give all, or at least to a very great majority, an interest in its preservation; to found it, as other things are founded, on men's interest. The stability of government requires that those who desire its continuance should be more powerful than those who desire its dissolution. This power, of course, is not always to be measured by mere numbers. Education, wealth, talents, are all parts and elements of the general aggregate of power. But numbers, nevertheless, constitute ordinarily the most important consideration, unless indeed there be a military force in the hands of the few by which they can control the many.

" It would seem, then, to be the part of political wisdom to found government on property, and to establish such distribution of property by the laws which regulate its transmission and alienation, as to interest the great majority of society in the protection of the government. This is, I imagine, the true theory and actual practice of our republican institutions. With property divided as we have it, no other government than that of a republic could be maintained, even were we foolish enough to desire it. There is reason, therefore, to expect a long continuance of our systems. Party and passion, doubtless, may prevail at times and much temporary mischief be done. Even modes and forms may be changed, and perhaps for the worse. But a great revolution in regard to property must take place before our governments can be moved from their republican basis, unless they be violently struck off by military power. The people possess the property more emphatically than it could ever be said of the people of any other country, and they can have no interest to overturn a government which protects that property by equal laws.

" If the nature of our institutions be to found government on property, and that it should look to those who hold property for its protection, it is entirely just that property should have its due weight and consideration in political arrangements. Life and personal liberty are, no doubt, to be protected by law; but property is also to be protected by law, and is the fund out of which the means for protecting life and liberty are usually furnished. We have no experience that teaches us that any other rights are safe where property is not safe. Confiscation and plunder are generally, in revolutionary commotions, not far before banishment, imprisonment, and death. It would be monstrous to give even the name of government to any association in which the rights of property should not be competently secured. The disastrous revolutions which the world has witnessed; those political thunderstorms and earthquakes which have overthrown the pillars of society from their very deepest foundations, have been revolutions *against property.*"

This argument prevailed with the convention, and no change was made in the property qualification for the office of governor, lieutenant-governor or senator. But the test oath was abolished, and the ballot given to every male citizen of full age who had lived one year in the state, and within two years preceding any election had paid a tax.

To this steady progress in the acquisition of the political rights of man the people of Rhode Island had hitherto remained indifferent, and still lived under the old charter granted by King Charles in 1663. But even Rhode Island now became infected with a longing for manhood suffrage, and in 1824, her first constitution was framed by a convention and rejected at the polls by her limited class of voters. Next came Maryland, where in 1826, after a contest covering more than twenty years, public offices were opened to the Jews. Since her constitution went into effect in 1776, every man appointed or elected to any office of profit or trust must, before he entered on his duties, subscribe a declaration of his belief in the Christian religion. Because of this restriction no Jew, nor any one else who did not believe in Christianity, could serve on a jury, or be a sheriff or an officer in the militia, or sit as a judge or magistrate, or practice law, or be a member of the assembly or the senate or hold even the humblest office in the state. Again and again attempts were made to break down this restriction, only to end in failure. But the time had now come when the rights of man were not to be any longer denied to non-Christians, when political equality was no longer to be confined to men of any sect or creed, when the old doctrine " all men are created equal " was to be applied to another great body of citizens. And in 1826, the " Jew Bill," as it was called, was once more introduced into the legislature.

" We take our stand," said the defenders of the bill, " on the Declaration of Independence. We hold these truths to be self-evident, that all men are created equal. The Jews are men and therefore created your equals. But do you treat them as such? No, for you say they are unworthy to sit by your side in the administration of a free government. They are endowed with certain inalienable rights, among which are life, liberty and the pursuit of happiness. But you have curtailed them in their liberty, you have hindered them in the pursuit of happiness, the best of all kinds of liberty — religious liberty, and the pursuit of eternal happiness — the best of all sorts of happiness. For the preservation of these, governments are instituted among men. But your government is instituted for their destruction. You put them under the ban of the republic. Says the Declaration of Independence, all governments derive their just powers from the consent of the governed. They never gave you their consent to deprive them of their civil and religious privileges. The bill now on your table gives to the Jews no new rights; it merely preserves to them rights which are immutably and inalienably theirs. If you continue to enforce this outlawry clause of your constitution, you rear up with the hand of arbitrary power, the worst of all measures, a religious hierarchy. The principles even upon which you uphold the pure Christian religion to the exclusion of every other, are the principles which upheld the Inquisition in Spain and the Episcopal hierarchy of England. The right to put up one religion is the right to put down another; the right to put down one is the right to put down all, and the right to put down all is the right to build up one on their ruins. A Jew may be president of the United States, yet he cannot be a constable in Maryland. A Jew may be judge of a United States district court, yet he cannot be an attorney of a county court of Maryland. A Jew may be a marshal of the United States, yet he cannot be a sheriff or clerk of a court in Maryland. Is this right? Was anything ever more cruel? Is this not a religious persecution? True, it is not the fagot or the rack, but is applied for the very same reason — because the religions of some men do not conform to that of the majority. An odious exclusion of one man from any of the benefits common to the rest of his fellow citizens, is a persecution differing only in degree but of a nature equally unjust with that whose instruments are chains and torture. In a land of equal rights, to be subjected to a degrading exception is a punishment of real severity.

"But, it is said, let this bill pass and we shall have Chinese, Turks and infidels in office. Is anybody really afraid that Chinese and Turks will be elected to office in Maryland? Is there any reason why they should not be, if the people think them worthy? I never saw but two Chinese in the United States, and they were servants of a New York merchant. I never saw but one Turk, and he was exhibited as a juggler. But the infidel! No religious test can have any effect on them. Will they hesitate to subscribe to the test if anything is to be gained by it? But this bill is not intended for Chinese, Turks or infidels. It is expressly intended for the Jews. And is not their religion of divine origin? Was not Christ a Jew? Do not we believe in the Old Testament?"

These arguments prevailed. The Jew Bill passed the legislature in 1825, the confirmatory act, as required by the constitution, passed in 1826, and the rights of man were yet further extended.

That an extreme should sooner or later be reached, that a part of the community, carried away by an eagerness to reform whatever in their opinion infringed the rights or restrained the liberties of man, should leave good sense behind and attempt the impossible, was inevitable. Individualism, the rights of the individual, now became a fad, and when in 1825, the great apostle of communism, Robert Owen, landed on our shores and began to preach the absolute equality of all men and all women, equality of rights, equality of labor, common ownership of property, and coöperation to the fullest extent, he found an all too ready audience and enthusiastic followers. That one man should have one hundred acres and another not a foot of land; that one man should have ten thousand dollars and another be in debt, was grossly unjust and bred that inequality which made the one man an aristocrat and the other a slave. Therefore all property should be held in common. That one man should be paid ten dollars a day for his services and another fifty cents was grossly unjust. Every form of labor, from the highest to the lowest, the skilled and the unskilled, was equally meritorious, honorable and deserving. Therefore the physician who could amputate a limb or by his skill save the life of a patient, was entitled to no more compensation than the man whose lot it was to dig ditches or carry a hod. The true community was that in which men and women dwelt in one great building, ate the same sort of food, shared the same amusements and wore the same sort of clothing, cut in the same fashion. When explaining his views to the audiences that gathered to hear Mr.

Owen as he went from city to city, it was his custom to begin by attempting to show that the construction of modern society was all wrong; that the prevalence of error, prejudice, vice and crime was due to the practice of bringing up the young in a system of society which he called the individual or selfish; and that there were two sets of circumstances which entirely regulated the formation of a man's character. The one was his religious belief, and the other was his education. Every child was possessed of a body and a mind over which he had no control; whether that mind was moulded for good or for ill depended on the circumstances with which the parents surrounded the child. "Had you," he would say, "on my right hand, been brought up under the influence of such circumstances as are to be found at the foot of the Rocky Mountains, you would all have been Indians, save as to the color of your skins. Had you, on my left hand, been exposed from infancy to the circumstances which prevail in China, you would have been Chinese, except in form and figure." Any social system, then, which ignored the power of circumstances was wrong. That system which was based on "the science of circumstances" was right. As to religion, it should be a rational one, founded on matter-of-fact and the evidences of the senses — in short, the revealed word of God. Any events recorded in books professing to be of divine origin which were in opposition to this principle were

false. The Scriptures were not divine nor written by men under divine influence, nor did they
more than any other writings contain the revealed
word or will of God. All religions, the Christian
included, were founded in error, and, so far from
being fitted to promote happiness and virtue
among mankind they had the opposite tendency.
If the human race, then, was to be made virtuous
and happy, the old system must be done away
with, for its intuitions and its prejudices could
not exist together with the principles of the new.

It was for this reason, therefore, that he urged
the formation of communities in which should be
associated persons in sympathy with his views.
The number in any community should never be
less than five hundred nor more than two thousand, and they should begin by purchasing a
tract of twenty thousand acres of good land. In
the center should be four buildings, each a thousand feet long, so placed as to form the four sides
of a hollow square. From the middle of each side
a building should project into the square and in it
should be the dining-hall, the kitchen, the laun-
dry, the store-rooms — in short, all the domestic
appliances needed for the comfort and conveni-
ence of those living in the dormitory to which it
was attached. The school-rooms, lecture-rooms,
laboratories, the chapels, concert-halls and ball-
rooms should be in the centers and corners of the
buildings. On the first and second stories should
be dormitories, and on the third floor the quarters

of unmarried persons and children over two years
of age, for at that time of life they were to be
taken from their parents lest they should acquire
the foolish ideas and habits of the old society.
Around the village thus arranged should lie the
farms. Every member should have equal rights
and privileges according to age, and be fully
supplied with the comforts and necessaries of life.
Nobody should own any land, or houses, or cattle,
for all property was to be held in common. There
should be no churches, no sects or creeds, no
religious worship, but moral lectures and such a
system of public education as would foster in the
young a love of justice, morality, and truth. For
the very young there should be dancing, singing
and military drill. For the older in years, such
studies as music and history, drawing and astron-
omy, geography, botany and agriculture. The
school-room should be, not a barn but a picture
gallery and museum. Learning should cease to
be a task and become a source of wonder and
delight.

That the people might have a practical illustra-
tion of the soundness of his views, Mr. Owen
bought from the Rappites their community town
of Harmony, in Indiana, and there before a motley gathering of men and women who had come
to share in his enterprise, he unfolded his plan for
the regeneration of society through coöperation.
He told them that it was idle to expect that men
trained as they had been should be able to pass

at one bound from an irrational to a rational system of society. A half-way house, a period of probation was necessary to fit them for the practice of coöperation; that he had determined, therefore, to form them into the Preliminary Society of New Harmony, give them a constitution which should continue for three years, and leave the management of affairs in the hands of a preliminary committee. But the committee sadly mis-managed affairs, and when a year had come and gone, Owen abolished the Preliminary Society, organized another which he called the New Harmony Community of Equality, and gave it a constitution which for those days was socialistic in the extreme. There was to be the utmost freedom of speech, absolute equality of rights and equality of duties, common ownership of property, a common treasury, and coöperation to the furthest extent. So far his followers were quite ready to go. But the next reform to be introduced bred trouble. First came a decree prescribing uniformity of dress. For men, the outer garments were to be a collarless jacket, drawn on over the head, pantaloons buttoned to the jacket, and a belt around the waist. The women were to wear pantalettes and a sleeveless frock that came down to the knees. Against this many of them openly rebelled, refused to wear the costume, and would have nothing to do with those who did. Still the great projector did not lose heart. Such things were but the fruit of the irrational system in which the human race had been trained since the first man set foot on the earth. They were painful and hard to endure, yet they must be borne with the patience of a reformer; and on the 4th of July, 1826, Owen went one step further and made a Declaration of Mental Independence which shocked and horrified far more people than it ever converted. Man, he said, up to that hour, all the world over had been a slave to a trinity of the most monstrous evils that could possibly be combined to inflict mental and physical evils on the whole race. One was private or individual ownership of property, another was absurd and irrational systems of religion, the third was the marriage tie which, he declared, ought to be made without any ceremony and terminated at the pleasure of those concerned. This was too much. His theories about property and coöperation, the arrangements of buildings, and the education of children were matters of opinion. In a land of toleration he might hold any religious belief or none. But the moment he touched the marriage rite he touched public morality, and his views were denounced from one end of the country to the other.

Hitherto the community had been singularly prosperous. Emigrants had come in so fast that to provide them with lodgings had been found impossible, and those contemplating settlement had been warned to wait. But now all was changed. Discord took the place of harmony, and before six months elapsed Owen was selling property to individuals, sign-boards were appearing, shops were opening, fences were going up, and New Harmony was taking on all the characteristics of a village of the unregenerated sort. Before a year had passed Owen, discouraged by the wreck he saw about him, bade his followers farewell and left them to their fate. But not before other communities of a like kind sprang up on the frontier. Some enthusiasts at Cincinnati, carried away by the eloquence of Owen, bought land and founded the Yellow Springs Community in Ohio. Others were started at Blue Springs, Indiana; at Kendal, near Canton, Ohio; at Pittsburg; at Coxsackie, New York; at Haverstraw, New York; at Valley Forge, Pennsylvania. Many of his followers went back to their old homes. Some were driven away as worthless. Others remained and formed little communities on the New Harmony lands. Two, his son Robert Dale Owen and his devoted admirer, Miss Fanny Wright, removed to New York to take part in the struggle for the rights of labor then under way in the East.

In the course of the two and twenty years which had elapsed since Congress laid the Long Embargo, our country had passed through a great industrial revolution. Manufactures had grown up, the tariffs of 1816, 1824, and 1828, had been enacted, protection to home industries had become the settled policy of the government, and the

Eastern, Middle and some of the Western states were dotted with mills, factories, machine shops, and manufacturing establishments of a hundred sorts. Great works of internal improvement were under way. Canals were being built, turnpikes constructed and railroad in course of building in a dozen states, and the great cities were being rebuilt. Hundreds of thousands of young men and women had been drawn from the farms to the mills and factories. A great body of machinists, skilled artisans, had come into existence, and tens of thousands of men from the old world had come over to fill the demand for unskilled labor. That these men should be content to live under the old conditions of labor was not to be expected. The long hours of labor, the liability to imprisonment for debt, which still lingered in many states, the need of a lien law, the impossibility of educating their children in a land where education counted for so much, were to them grievances of a serious kind. The first quarter of the nineteenth century, therefore, had scarcely passed when a great movement began in the manufacturing states for the rights of labor. Social unions of various crafts were formed in all the seaboard cities north of Baltimore, and began to agitate for labor reforms. In 1828, an attempt was made in the New York Legislature to secure a mechanics' lien law, and a report strongly favoring such a measure of relief was presented. In Philadelphia the workingmen, breaking old ties, entered politics on their own behalf and formed a labor party. At a public meeting in August it was formally resolved to urge the workingmen to support no candidate for a seat in the legislature or in the city councils who would not pledge himself to further the interests and demands of " the working classes," and a call was issued for organization. The city and county were marked off into four districts, from each of which delegates were sent to a general convention which nominated assemblymen, common councilmen, and auditor.

The tickets were defeated, but the organization continued, and ere another year went by made two demands for reform: one that the managers of the House of Refuge who had just introduced mechanical occupations into their institution, should see to it that the mechanics and workingmen of Philadelphia suffered no injury, and another that the State of Pennsylvania should establish a system of free republican schools, open to children of the rich and of the poor without distinction.

Judged by the standard of public instruction as now maintained in Pennsylvania, the demand of the workingmen was reasonable and just. The constitution of the commonwealth, framed a generation before, required that the children of the poor should be educated at the public cost. The injunction was mandatory; the meaning was plain. Yet no steps were taken to carry it out till 1809, when a law was enacted requiring the assessors of taxes to make a census of the children whose parents were too poor to educate them, send the boys and girls to the nearest school, and assess the cost on the taxpayers. Even this wise provision was neglected. Some districts had no schools of any kind; in others the funds were embezzled, misapplied, perverted, or the law but partly executed, for the people refused to accept the benefit conferred lest their children should be looked on and treated as paupers. Meanwhile the cities increased in population, and the number of children growing up in absolute ignorance became so large that in 1818 a second step forward was taken and the city and county of Philadelphia, the city and borough of Lancaster, and the city of Pittsburg were formed into three districts, with free schools in which children whose parents were too poor to educate them were taught reading, writing, arithmetic and geography. No child whose parents could pay his schooling was admitted, and this in the eyes of the workingmen was an offensive class distinction. It separated the children of the rich from those of the poor and said to the latter, " You are paupers." That some men should be rich and others poor was inevitable, but to build up class hatred was not necessary, and no surer way of preventing it could be devised than a system of equal republican education with free schools open to the children of all citizens alike.

The efforts which workingmen were thus making to secure great social reforms, and especially their demands for free public schools, now warmly enlisted in their cause another body of reformers known as the Free Enquirers, who were regarded at that day by conservative people with the same horror and detestation that anarchists and socialists are regarded in ours.

The center of this movement was New York City, and there, in October 1829, the workingmen were summoned to meet and organize for the defence of their rights, and as the fall elections were about to take place, to put into the field candidates of their own party. Hundreds responded, a great meeting was held, and before adjourning a committee of fifty was appointed to report a plan of organization and write an address. At another meeting held a month later, an assembly ticket was chosen and a set of resolutions which did duty as a labor-party platform were adopted. They read as follows:

" 1. In the opinion of this meeting, the first appropriation of the soil of the state to private and exclusive possession was eminently unjust.

"2. That it was substantially feudal in its character, inasmuch as those who received enormous and unequal possessions were lords, and those who received little or nothing were vassals.

" 3. That hereditary transmission of wealth on the one hand and of poverty on the other has brought down to the present generation all the evils of the feudal system; and all this, in our opinion is the prime source of all our calamities.

" 4. In this view of the matter, that the greatest impostors, knaves and paupers of the age are our bankers, who swear they have promised to pay to their debtors thirty or thirty-five million dollars on demand, at the same time that they have, as they also swear, only three or four millions to do it with.

" 5. That more than one hundred broken banks within a few years past admonish the community to destroy banks altogether.

" 6. That more than a thousand kinds of counterfeit notes from five hundred to a single dollar give double force to the admonition.

" 7. That exemption is privilege, and as such the exemption from taxation of churches and church property and the property of priests to an amount not exceeding fifteen hundred dollars, is a direct and positive robbery of the people."

The seriousness of this movement and the eagerness with which laborers, mechanics, clerks, men who belonged to every class of the great body of toilers, hastened to give it encouragement and support, now brought into existence a new journal, and in October 1829, the first number of *The Workingman's Advocate* made its appearance. " We think," said the prospectus of the *Advocate*, " we see in the existing state of society around us something radically wrong. We see one portion living in luxury and idleness. We see another engaged in employments which are useless or worse than useless. We see a third part — and it is the most numerous — groaning under the oppression and miseries inflicted on it by the other two, and we see all suffering from the effects of vice produced by luxury and indolence, and of ignorance caused by poverty. We are therefore opposed to monopolies, exemptions, exclusive privileges. We consider it an exclusive privilege for one part of the community to have the means of education in college while another is restricted to the common schools, or forced by dire poverty to have no education at all. We are therefore in favor of a system of education equally open to all men.'' On the same principle the *Advocate* was opposed to banks in general and to the Bank of the United States in particular, was against imprisonment for debt, against the ownership of land in large quantities by private individuals, and in favor of a lien law, and heartily supported the ticket the committee of fifty had placed before the voters.

It was then the custom in New York to open the polls on three consecutive days. At the close of the first day it seemed so likely that the Workingmen's Ticket would triumph that the journals which upheld the Republican cause called loudly on the friends of good order to rally. '' The general impression prevails,'' said one newspaper, '' that the ticket for assembly got up by the disciples of Fanny Wright, and wrongfully called

the Mechanics' Ticket, has received a large proportion of the votes given yesterday. Some have
declared that it is far ahead of every other. Be
this as it may, it becomes the friends of good
order in this community, of whatever party, to
go to the polls and by their votes prevent so
shameful a result. Shameful it would be if even
a moderate support were given to tickets prepared
by persons who scoff at morality and demand a
system of public robbery." "We understand,"
said another, "with astonishment and alarm that
the ' Infidel Ticket,' miscalled ' the Workingmen's
Ticket,' is far ahead of every other assembly
ticket in the city. What a state of things have
we reached! A ticket got up openly and avowedly
in opposition to all banks, in opposition to social
order, in opposition to the rights of property,
running ahead of every other! Is not this sufficient to startle men who have regard for the
fundamental laws of society?" On the second
and third days the friends of religion and order
thus appealed to did rally, and but one candidate
on the Mechanics' Ticket, Ebenezer Ford, was
elected.

The great vote cast for Ford — 6,166 — alarmed
the community. All the horrors of anarchy
seemed at hand. The "Fanny Wright Ticket,"
the "Infidel Ticket" was denounced and the
legislature called on to unseat Mr. Ford. The
leaders of this miscalled mechanics' party, the
people were told, held that everything was wrong

in the present state of society, and that the whole
system must be changed. Their object was
represented to be to turn the state into an Owenite
community, confiscate all land and hold it for the
general use of the people, strike down religion,
and abolish marriage.

So horrid a picture of socialism disturbed the
mechanics, who now made haste to publicly disa-
vow all connection with Owen, with Fanny
Wright and the Free Enquirers, and at a ward
meeting passed resolutions denying all sympathy
with the " Infidel party," repelling with scorn
the charge that they were hostile to the civil,
moral and religious institutions of the country,
and declaring agrarian laws to be debasing,
wicked and dishonest. The New York Typo-
graphical Society went further yet and appointed
a committee to report as to who Owen was and
in what his scheme consisted. The committee
assured the typesetters that Robert Dale Owen
was a Scotchman, that he probably had never
been naturalized, and that he had been assisted
in his labors " by one Fanny Wright, also an
exotic of some notoriety."

" It does seem unaccountably strange," said
the report, " that a native of that part of the
world where thousands are every day groaning
under oppression, should leave these unfortunates,
come over to the New World, and, in the midst
of a people enjoying the fullest liberty proclaim
himself the apostle of equal rights and tender

them the hand of friendship against their oppres-
sors. Such insolence might well be treated with
contempt were it not for the fact that a band of
choice spirits of foreign origin, have united and,
taking advantage of our mild laws, are sowing
the seeds of discontent and rebellion. It is true
that there is some distress among laboring people.
It is true that labor is not as well paid as in times
past, that a man working with his hands is now
unable to earn as much as he once could. But
in our country, at least, the distress is caused not
by anything Owen could reform, but by the introduction of labor-saving machinery during the last
thirty years. Has Owen any remedy to propose?
Far from it. He calls on the workingmen to
associate for defence of their rights when no
rights are endangered.'' The report ended with
a repudiation of his plan and a denial of all sympathy with his purposes. The Painters' Society,
on the other hand, took a different view, admitted
that much Mr. Owen said was true, and was disposed to favor his plan for free education. At
Philadelphia, where the workingmen supported a
ticket at the October election for city and county
officers, they too denied the charge of sympathy
with Miss Wright as warmly as their fellow-
laborers in New York. '' We view,'' so ran a
resolution adopted at a public meeting after the
election, '' the report charging us with being
disciples of Miss Wright, and connecting religious
points with our contention, as a base fabrication

propagated by our enemies. We disclaim all
adherence to Miss Wright's principles and hold
them foreign to our views, and appeal to the fact
of the existence of the Workingmen's party on
the principles it now professes for nearly a year
before she appeared among us.''

But it mattered little whether the workingmen
avowed or disavowed sympathy with the Free
Enquirers; the fact remained that a serious
reform movement was well under way and was
spreading and gaining in importance daily. All
over the country journals were appearing to advocate it, and societies were forming to labor in its
behalf. In New York City the *Telescope* was
busy exposing the designs of the clergy and holding up to view the dangers of ecclesiastical
encroachment. At Rochester the *Spirit of the
Age* was denouncing imprisonment for debt and
capital punishment, and calling loudly for a
mechanics' lien law. At Canton, in Ohio, the
Farmers' and Mechanics' Society of Stark County
had been founded to spread the new doctrines
and agitate for coöperation and reform. At St.
Louis there was a Society of Free Enquirers. In
Alabama '' The Ladies' Bill,'' to give women the
right to hold after marriage property which
belonged to them before, was warmly debated in
the legislature, and in Tuscaloosa another *Spirit
of the Age* upheld the cause of the people as
vigorously as its Rochester contemporary. The
Southern Free Press of Charleston, South Carolina,

announced its principles to be " No sect, no creed; open to all," and declared that it would collect such information as was useful to mechanics and workingmen and would look to them for support. " Our great object," said the editor in his prospectus, " will be to urge you to break down the barrier which separates your children from those of lordly aristocrats by the establishment of national schools." At New Castle, in Delaware, an Association of Working People was formed with a membership open to any person twenty-one years of age who was engaged in any branch of productive labor. " How is it," said the preamble to their constitution, " that all classes save the laboring are heard in the legislature? The commercial, the agricultural, the manufacturing, ask for protection and it is granted. But what is accorded the workingman — nothing. Yet who needs protection more? The price of labor is hourly going down because of the numbers thrown out of employment by labor-saving machinery. The cost of every article of consumption, meantime, is increased by taxation. ' Does not the present system, under such circumstances, tend to increase the poverty of the poor and add to the riches of the rich?' Let us then be represented in the legislature. Let us unite at the polls and give our votes to no candidate who is not pledged to support a rational system of education to be paid for out of the public funds, and to further a rightful protection for the laborer." At Wil-

mington, Delaware, was another *Free Press* like-
wise pledged "to be open to all for the free,
chaste and temperate discussion of subjects connected with the welfare of the human family."
Its mission was "to arouse the attention of
workingmen to the importance of coöperation in
order to attain the rank and station in society to
which they are justly entitled by virtue of industry, but from which they are excluded by want
of a system of equal republican education." In
New York City two new journals of a strongly
agrarian sort began their career early in 1830.
The one, *The Friend of Equal Rights*, demanded
the equal division of property among the adults
of a family at the age of maturity. The other,
the *Daily Sentinel*, was devoted "to the interests
of mechanics and other workingmen," and at
once became a political power. Indeed, it was
started for the sole purpose of becoming such a
power.

The late election in the city made it clear that
the workingmen had, in the language of our time,
bolted their party, had supported a ticket which
was not put forward by any political faction, and
had done so because they were discontented and
because they did not believe that their grievances
would ever be removed by the men then in
power. Six thousand votes cast solidly for or
against any of the three parties then struggling
for control in the city and state was too serious a
matter to be treated lightly, and each of the three

began to strive eagerly for the support of the workingman.

From the city the movement spread to the state, where it was taken up by the leaders of every one of the innumerable knots of anti-regency, anti-Van Buren, Anti-masonic and Clay Republicans. At the charter election in Albany, in the spring of 1830, the workingmen united on a ticket and carried four wards out of five. In Troy the same course was pursued, and " not one regency man," it was boastfully said, was elected.

A little later the Friends of Liberal and Moral Principles met at Rochester. They were, their original resolution set forth, opposed to kingcraft, priestcraft, monopolies, interference of missionaries, sectarian tracts, Sunday mails, union of church and state, and imprisonment for debt. To prove their sincerity on this latter point the deputy jailer was asked to release all persons confined in the county prison for debt and send the bill to the convention, which was accordingly done.

In 1832, a convention of workingmen assembled in the State House, attended by delegates from New York and all the New England States save Vermont. The issues discussed were the ten-hour day, the effect of banks and other monopolies on the condition of the laboring classes, the improvement of the system of education, legislation for the improvement of factories, abolition of imprisonment for debt, extension of the right of suffrage, taxation, and a lien law.

Associations of workmen of every sort, demands for a ten-hour day and better wages, and strikes when they were refused, now became a feature of the times. Again and again the strikers were prosecuted for conspiracy. Sometimes the courts held for the workmen, more often they were found guilty and fined under the common law of England.

To the conservative part of the community these demands seemed revolutionary. Yet each one of them was long since granted as a right. State after state enacted a lien law. The common school as we know it, a school maintained by the city or the state and open alike to the children of the rich and the poor, was soon to be found in almost every state. And when, in 1840, Van Buren by proclamation put the ten-hour day in force over all public works, the struggle for shorter hours was practically over.

The old struggle against monopolies, however, went on and in New York bred a party which took the name of Equal Righters. The faces of these men were set against every custom, usage, institution, law which gave to any corporation, association, company or individual any privilege, exemption or right not enjoyed by the humblest man in the state. A bank could issue non-interest-bearing notes that passed as currency and were taken by the state and the people in payment of taxes and the discharge of debts. No private man could enjoy such a privilege; therefore a bank was an oppressive monopoly, curtailing the rights and liberties of man. A railroad, a canal company having the right of eminent domain could take the land of the farmer against his will, and force him to accept such compensation as others thought proper. No individual could do this; therefore canal and railroad companies were monopolies and infringed the rights of man to acquire and hold property. The exemption of church property from taxation, the concentration of capital in industrial corporations, the holding of immense estates, the accumulations of great fortunes were all unjust discriminations against the individual, hostile to equal rights, and ought to be abolished or prevented.

These, it is true, were the opinions of extremists. But beneath them all are clearly discernible the inalienable rights for which our fathers fought — the rights of life, liberty and the pursuit of happiness. Their work was but one of the many phases of the ceaseless struggle for the rights of man.

How serious this struggle might become, to what lengths the people might go to secure their rights is well illustrated in the Dorr War in Rhode Island in the early forties.

When the colonies began to take up civil government and framed their first written constitutions, the people of Rhode Island were living under the charter granted by King Charles in 1663, which was not in any way modified when

that colony, having declared itself free and independent, ratified the Declaration of Independence
July 19, 1776. The machinery of government
consisted of a governor chosen by the people at
large, ten assistants also elected by the freemen
at large, and seventy deputies or representatives,
two each from twenty-six towns, four from Providence, Portsmouth and Warwick, and six from
Newport. The charter did not specify what
should be the suffrage qualification. The General
Assembly did this by repeated acts, and from
1798 to 1842, the qualifications were a freehold of
lands or tenements worth one hundred and thirty-
four dollars, or yielding an annual rental of seven
dollars, or the eldest son of a freeholder. Until
1776, the assistants and deputies sat as one body.
After that year they sat as separate bodies in
different characters, and the assistants were re-
named senators. From time to time, as in 1777,
1797, 1811 and 1817, half-hearted efforts were
made to secure a constitution and extend the suffrage, but the people took no interest in the issue
and they failed. The agitations of 1820, 1821, 1822
and 1823, were purely the work of the newspapers.
No popular demand whatever was made, and the
constitution of 1824, when framed was rejected by
the voters. But the tariffs of 1824 and 1828, produced a marked change in Rhode Island. Mills
and factories increased with astonishing rapidity.
Certain towns and cities became centers of manufactures, and drew into them thousands of opera-

tives, who, having no freeholds, could neither be eligible to office nor cast a vote. The discontent of these people found expression in 1829 in petitions to the Assembly from Warren, Bristol and Providence, and brought from a committee of the legislature a most singular report.

"The right of suffrage," said the report, "as it is the origin and basis of every free elective government, so it is the peculiar and exclusive prerogative of the people, and cannot without infringing that prerogative be subjected to any other control than that of the people themselves. Our ancestors thought fit to preserve the liberties of themselves and their posterity by limiting the franchise to the sound part of the community, the substantial freeholders of the state. Had they not a right to adopt these provisions? And have not their descendants and those whom they have associated with them in conformity to those provisions equally a right to preserve and adhere to them? Complainers mistake their right, *which is a right to qualify* themselves as the law directs, not a right to be voters without such qualification."

The report then goes on to defend the freehold qualification and denounce democracy as the curse of every nation which has ever yielded to its charms.

The blow thus delivered by the legislative committee ended for the time being all agitation for a liberal suffrage, and five years passed before the issue was raised once more. This time the question was taken up by two towns in the north end of Providence county, which invited all towns in the state to send delegates to a convention to be held at Providence. Ten responded and by the convention thus assembled a committee was appointed to write an Address to the People of Rhode Island.

The writer of the report was Thomas W. Dorr, who took the ground that when the colonies severed the political ties which bound them to Great Britain, all obligation to obey a British charter or a constitution of government was of course dissolved; that the sovereignty of the king then passed, not to the governor and company of Rhode Island but to the people at large, and that the people thus acquired the undoubted right to establish a constitution of their own making. As no such government was then established, the people are urged by Mr. Dorr to choose representatives to a convention to frame a liberal and permanent constitution.

Once more the legislature, now somewhat alarmed, issued a call for a convention which met in September 1834, adjourned till November, and then again till February 1835, at which time its members failed to appear. And so the matter rested till the great Whig campaign of 1840 shook the country and made even Rhode Island a Whig state and gave her a Whig senator in Congress. In the midst of the famous Log Cabin and Hard

Cider campaign there was suddenly scattered broadcast over the state a pamphlet purporting to come from The First Social Reform Society of New York, but undoubtedly written in Rhode Island. It was called "An Address to the Citizens of Rhode Island who are Denied the Right of Suffrage," and urged them to hold primary meetings in each town, call a convention, name the time and place of meeting, elect delegates, and append to the credentials of each member a list of the voters. The convention was then to canvass the votes, and if the whole number cast was found to exceed that cast at the last general election for Representatives to Congress, then the convention was to consider itself a representative of the majority of the people and fully authorized to frame a constitution. Under this constitution members of Congress were to be elected and go to Washington to claim their seats. The burden would then be thrust upon Congress to decide whether the charter of 1663, or the constitution formed by the people of Rhode Island was a true republican form of government.

Acting under these suggestions, a Rhode Island Suffrage Association was formed at Providence in the autumn of 1840, an example which was so promptly followed that by the spring of 1841, there was a suffrage society in nearly every town in the state. The Declaration of Principles issued by the Suffrage Association of Societies set forth:

1. That all men are created free and equal.

2. That property should not give political advantages to its possessors.

3. That every body politic should have for its basis a bill of rights and a written constitution.

4. That Rhode Island has neither.

5. That the charter was void when Rhode Island became independent.

6. That every state is entitled to a republican form of government.

7. That the majority should govern.

8. That the time for submission to unjust outrages on social and political rights had gone by.

So far neither the Whigs nor the Democratic party gave any countenance to the movement. But the Whig triumph angered the Democrats, whose leading newspaper took occasion to remark that there were fourteen thousand men in Rhode Island who were not allowed to vote for president, that the election might have been different had these men voted, and that its columns were open to a discussion of a freer suffrage. But the suffragists declined the offer, started a new paper of their own, and at once began a campaign of education. Public meetings were held for debates on the many questions growing out of the issue. A great street parade with banners, badges and mottoes was held in Providence, and in May of 1841, a convention of suffragists gathered at Newport, and when it adjourned ordered the next meeting to be held at Providence on July 5, 1841, at which time and place a call was issued for a people's convention to frame a constitution, and a pledge given that if such constitution so made should be adopted by a majority of the people it should be sustained and carried into effect by any means necessary. But the legislature in the meantime had acted on sundry petitions from freeholders and had called a convention, the delegates to which were to be chosen by the freeholders. There were then two such bodies, one the creature of the legislature, known as the Freeholders' Convention, the other the creature of the people, known as the People's Convention. Here was a deliberate exercise of the right asserted in the Declaration of Independence that governments are instituted among men to secure the rights of man, and that when they fail to accomplish the purpose for which they are instituted it is the right of the people to alter or abolish them.

With the details of the work of these conventions we are not concerned. It is enough to know that from the People's Convention came a constitution providing for almost universal suffrage, and from the Freemen's Convention a constitution was submitted by which suffrage was limited to possessors of one hundred and thirty-four dollars' worth of land or five hundred dollars' worth of taxable property. Both conventions limited the right to vote on questions of taxation to payers of a property tax. Each convention then adjourned to meet again after the people had voted on the constitution it favored.

The result as to the people's constitution was announced, in January 1842, to be ratification by a large majority, and that the constitution therefore ought to be and was the paramount law and constitution of the State of Rhode Island and Providence Plantations.

In March 1842, the people were called on to vote on the freemen's constitution. Sixteen thousand seven hundred and two votes were cast — 8,013 for and 8,689 against it, and it was defeated. So stood the contest when the General Assembly, in April 1842, enacted a law " In Relation to Offenses against the State," but really against the people's constitution. After a preamble declaring that certain designing persons had framed and were attempting to put in operation a plan to subvert the government of the state, it was enacted that all meetings for the election of state officers other than those provided for by law were illegal and void; that moderators, wardens and clerks of such meetings would be deemed guilty of misdemeanors and fined and imprisoned, and that persons taking a state office because of such election would be guilty of treason and imprisoned for life. The suffragists dubbed this the Algerine Law, and went on with their elections under their constitution. Thomas W. Dorr was chosen governor, Amasa Eddy, Jr., lieutenant-governor, and other party leaders were made secretary of state, general treasurer, and attorney-general. A general assembly was also chosen.

Two days later the Charter election took place, when Samuel W. King was elected governor.

Under the Algerine Law one hundred and eighty persons by their acts had made themselves liable to arrest and punishment. Five had been elected to general offices of state, eighty-nine were members of the house, and twelve of the senate, and the rest were sheriffs or had acted as moderators or clerks of the elections. The question then was, will the charter government arrest these men or quietly suffer the people's government to go into operation? The question was still unanswered when May 3d came, and in the presence of a great crowd of citizens the People's General Assembly took possession of an unfinished foundry in Providence, organized, listened to the inaugural address of Governor Dorr, and after a session of two days adjourned to meet again in July.

May 4th the Charter Assembly gathered at Newport and resolved that, " Whereas, a portion of the people had formed a pretended constitution and had met in lawless assemblages and elected state officers, and had organized executive and legislative departments of government; therefore, there existed in the State of Rhode Island an insurrection against the constituted authority, and that a requisition should be made by the legislature on the President of the United States forthwith to interpose the authority and power of the United States to protect the state from domestic violence.''

Acting under the instructions, Governor King at once sent off the requisition to President Tyler, and on the same day a similar cry for help was despatched to the president by Governor Dorr, who promptly followed his messengers to Washington. Scarcely was he out of the state when arrests for treason began, and in course of three days seven of the People's party were under bonds to stand trial. Alarmed at this show of energy other members of the Dorr government began, one by one, to resign, and the report was circulated that Dorr had fled the state.

This rumor was false, and on May 15th, Dorr, on his way back from Washington, reached Stonington, Connecticut, and was escorted thence to Providence by some two hundred of his party, spoke from a carriage to an audience of several thousand, and made his headquarters in the house of one of his followers. Some cannon belonging to the state were now seized, and about midnight on May 17th, an armed band of Dorrites having come in from Woonsocket, orders were issued to attack the arsenal. Before dawn, accordingly, the little army with Dorr in command wound its way through the city streets, drew up before the arsenal, made a demand for its surrender, and when this was refused twice attempted to fire on the building with cannon. Each time there was a flash in the pan, and after these dismal failures the little army began to dissolve, and Dorr, with a few followers dragged the useless guns back to headquarters. There he was informed that all members of his government living in Providence had resigned, and he fled to Woonsocket, and then to New York.

More resignations now followed, and the People's Government seemed in a state of collapse. The governor had fled, the legislature could not have mustered a quorum, and no state officer was attempting to attend to the duties of his office.

But the end was not yet. Encouraged by friends in New York, Dorr returned, gathered a few followers at the little town of Chepatchet, near the Connecticut border, and began to fortify a camp on a spot called Acote's Hill. Against this the state forces now move with great deliberation, to find when they reached the spot that Dorr had fled and his army melted away. Then the state authorities grew bold. Hundreds of arrests were made, martial law was declared, Dorr was proclaimed a traitor, one thousand and then five thousand dollars' reward was offered for his arrest, and requisitions for his return were made on the governors of neighboring states. During more than a year Dorr remained a fugitive, but at last in 1843, he returned to Providence, was arrested, tried, found guilty of treason and sentenced to imprisonment for life. This, in the opinion of the people, was wholly unnecessary severity. A movement for his liberation was started and carried to the polls, and on this issue a " liberation " governor was elected, and in June 1845, Dorr was set free. In 1851, the legislature restored to him civil and political rights, and in 1854, reviewed and annulled the judgment of the Supreme Court of Rhode Island and ordered the clerk to write across the record of the judgment the words " Reversed and annulled by order of the General Assembly." Long ere this time his efforts bore fruit, and in 1843, Rhode Island framed a written constitution which forbade slavery and liberalized the franchise.

And here we may safely leave the subject. The story of the yet greater struggle for the rights of man during the last half of the century is too long and too complicated to be even summarized. It is enough to know that the rights of the black man, the rights of children, the rights of women, the rights of workingmen have received in the last fifty years a recognition never before given them. The free common school, the wise system of factory legislation, the reduction of the working day from sixteen hours to ten and even eight, the abolition of slavery, the gradual opening to the women of the professions of law and medicine, and of innumerable fields of labor from which, fifty years ago they were absolutely shut out, have produced an amount of human happiness which it is not possible to rightly estimate.

It is enough to know that the principles laid down by our forefathers have not been repudiated;

that we have, by a steady, well-ordered progress been drawing nearer and nearer to the conditions of life our forefathers so fondly pictured; that at no time in our history has life been held more sacred, liberty been less restrained, the opportunities for the pursuit of happiness so many. Never did our government so nearly derive its just powers from the consent of the governed, and never did the governed so fully recognize as self-evident truths the three inalienable rights of man.